A Smart Agriculture Land Suitability Detection Model Using Machine Learning with Google Earth Engine

Muhammad Umer
Rana M. Amir Latif
Muhammad Farhan
Noor Zaman Jhanjhi
Mamoona Humayun
Syed Jawad Hussain

ELIVA PRESS

ELIVA PRESS

Muhammad Umer
Rana M. Amir Latif
Muhammad Farhan
Noor Zaman Jhanjhi
Mamoona Humayun
Syed Jawad Hussain

The development and growth of plants and crops heavily depend on the number of mineral nutrients and their concentrations available in the soil, moisture in the soil, air quality and water availability. Plants or crops sometimes face challenges in obtaining a sufficient amount of nutrients for the necessary cellular process from the soil due to immobility. The decrease in crops' growth, fertility, or poor food quality happens due to deficiency of natural nutrients, soil moisture, and water, which is required to meet the demand of plants' necessary cellular processes. Lack of nutrients in the soil may result in biodiversity reduction, which directly affects most food webs. This proposed research study will focus on the development of the agriculture land assessment model. Google Earth Engine is a publicly available data repository that hosts an enormous variety of datasets, including climate and weather forecasts, landcover, environmental variables, non-optical and optical wavelengths, water history and classification, and air quality. Precise high spatial resolution cropland extent product up to 60m resolution of very large or even of a specific region of any country is considered very important in addressing several challenges of water security and global food. Cropland products typically cover limited or broad farm areas that are critical for developing specific, higher-level cropland products such as crop irrigation, crop water production, crop intensities, and crop varieties methods. The processing by constructing precision-high resolution cropland-wide training and testing data on diverse geographical locations and safe frontiers, computing capacity, and the management of vast volumes of geographical data are all called challenges. A high-resolution cropland product derived from Sentinel-2 Multispectral (Level-1C) data for different characteristics of Pakistan was produced for the analysis. In this analysis, eight separate Sentinel-2 multi-spectral instruments (level-1C) data from 2018-19 (SWIR 2, SWIR 1, Cirrus, NIR, Red, Green, Blue, and Aerosols) have been used. The pixel-based classification algorithms have been used, and their precision is measured and seen in this study; both computations and analyzes have been conducted.

Published: Eliva Press SRL
Address: MD-2060, bd.Cuza-Voda, 1/4, of. 21 Chişinău, Republica
Moldova
Email: info@elivapress.com
Website: www.elivapress.com

ISBN: 978-1-63648-012-1

A Smart Agriculture Land Suitability Detection Model Using Machine Learning with Google Earth Engine

[1]Muhammad Umer
[2]Rana M. Amir Latif
[3]Muhammad Farhan
[4]Noor Zaman Jhanjhi
[5]Mamoona Humayun
[6]Syed Jawad Hussain
muhammadumer063@gmail.com[1]
ranaamir10611@gmail.com[2]
farhansajid@gmail.com[3]
noorzaman.jhanjhi@taylors.edu.my[4]
mahumayun@ju.edu.sa[5]
Jawad@biit.edu.pk[6]

ABSTRACT

The development and growth of plants and crops heavily depend on the number of mineral nutrients and their concentrations available in the soil, moisture in the soil, air quality and water availability. Plants or crops sometimes face challenges in obtaining a sufficient amount of nutrients for the necessary cellular process from the soil due to immobility. The decrease in crops' growth, fertility, or poor food quality happens due to deficiency of natural nutrients, soil moisture, and water, which is required to meet the demand of plants' necessary cellular processes. Lack of nutrients in the soil may result in biodiversity reduction, which directly affects most food webs. This proposed research study will focus on the development of the agriculture land assessment model. Google Earth Engine is a publicly available data repository that hosts an enormous variety of datasets, including climate and weather forecasts, landcover, environmental variables, non-optical and optical wavelengths, water history and classification, and air quality. Precise high spatial resolution cropland extent product up to 60m resolution of very large or even of a specific region of any country is considered very important in addressing several challenges of water security and global food. Cropland products typically cover limited or broad farm areas that are critical for developing specific, higher-level cropland products such as crop irrigation, crop water production, crop intensities, and crop varieties methods. The processing by constructing precision-high resolution cropland-wide training and testing data on diverse geographical locations and safe frontiers, computing capacity, and the management of vast volumes of geographical data are all called challenges. A high-resolution cropland product derived from Sentinel-2 Multispectral (Level-1C) data for different characteristics of Pakistan was produced for the analysis. In this analysis, eight separate Sentinel-2 multi-spectral instruments (level-1C) data from 2018-19 (SWIR 2, SWIR 1, Cirrus, NIR, Red, Green, Blue, and Aerosols) have been used. The pixel-based classification algorithms have been used, and their precision is measured and seen in this study; both computations and analyzes have been conducted on the cloud-based Google Earth Engine computing network. In cropland building, after applying time-composite property in 4-6 intervals over one year, each band's median value was used, which contributed to a mega-data-cube of 32-48 capes. Training and testing data were obtained from the Google Earth Engine map console at a high spatial 10 m resolution for this analysis. The basis of research information for the testing of the computer algorithms consists of 855 training samples, which culminated in a manufacturing field of 200 individual validation samples measuring product accuracy. The 10 m to 60 m of Pakistan's cropland scale commodity demonstrated the best overall validation accuracy of 82% with an 89% accuracy by the manufacturer and 77% by the customer in the CART algorithm compared to the validation accuracy of three other Support Vector Machine, Random Forest, and Naïve Bayes algorithms. Their validity is lowest. Pakistan's average cropland areas were calculated to be 370,200 m2, and the croplands scale of goods indicated that subnational croplands could be measured. The research offers a conceptual change in the development of cropland maps utilizing remote sensing multi-date.

Keywords

Geospatial Analysis, Big Data Analysis, Machine Learning, Data Mining, Google Earth Engine, Cloud Computing, Cropland Mapping, Sentinel-2 MSI

Table of Contents

List of Figures

List of Tables

List of Abbreviations

GEE Google Earth Engine
IDE Integrated Development Environment
IDF Inverse Term Frequency
GP Google Play
D3S Driver Drowsiness Detection System
IAP In Application Purchases
NB Naïve Bayes

1 Introduction

1.1 Overview

The backbone of Pakistan's economy is the agriculture and the agriculture sector directly support the country's population food need. Also, 26% of Pakistan's gross domestic production (GDP) depends on the agriculture sector (Rehman et al., 2015). Further, agriculture is considered an essential factor behind the economy's growth and the reduction of poverty. Agriculture sectors in Pakistan are providing employment opportunities to the people, promoting infrastructure creation, helping in the supply of raw materials for manufacturing products for several uses, and, most notably agriculture sector generates foreign exchange for the country.

The development and growth of plants and crops heavily depend on the number of mineral nutrients and their concentrations available in the soil. Plants or crops sometimes face challenges in obtaining a sufficient amount of nutrients for the soil's necessary cellular process due to immobility. The decrease in crop growth, fertility, or poor food quality happens due to deficiency of natural nutrients requires to meet the demand of plants necessary cellular process. Lack of nutrients in the soil may result in biodiversity reduction, which directly affects most food webs. The reason for changes in the availability of different nutrients in soil occurs due to change in climate and atmosphere, and these changes are seriously affecting the plant's growth in a healthy manner (Lal, 2016). New strategies or technologies should need to be adopted to cope with all these obstacles mentioned above. Soil quality is an essential factor in agriculture, and mineral nutrients are usually obtained from the soil. Some plants cannot absorb nutrients from the soil due to soil composition and chemistry, resulting in lower production. Some fruits or vegetables grow more effectively in specific soil types because their structural features and possess mechanisms are well adapted to nutrient-limited soils. Growth of crops and plants also depends on geographic distribution, less than ideal environment situation affects the growth/production of crops. Identifying suitable land for agriculture activities is now considered an essential phase before the development of any cropland. Suitable cropland not only enhance productivity, but it also improves the life and freshness of plants and crops. Extreme temperature affecting plant development and growth, also soil water deficits increase the temperature effects on plants (Hatfield and Prueger, 2015). Soil moisture is also an essential factor behind the growth of plants. In any land area which remains dry for more than six days, the seeds are assumed to be dead.

Vegetables and fruits are common and inexpensive sources of vitamins and minerals; these are standard components of the human diet. The growing concept of 'Balanced Diet' consumption of vegetables is also growing day by day. The concentrations of toxic gases in the air grow due to an increase in population, and traffic on the road.

These toxic gases not only affecting human health but also damaging the growth and freshness of fruits and vegetables. In poor air quality, the presence of various atmospheric pollutants continuously damaging plants and crops, and mostly plants drop their leaves earlier before their full growth due to toxic air (Asseng et al., 2015).

Based on the factors discussed above, identification of land suitability is very important for healthy growth and better production of crops, vegetables, and fruits. Land suitability for agriculture activities can be found through time series analysis of air quality or toxic gases in the air, soil moisture, temperature, and water history of understudy land area.

Agriculture land suitability evaluation requires temperature, soil moisture, water history, and air quality, which is time-series data. Based on the analysis of these data through machine learning techniques, a prediction model can be constructed to predict the suitability of land for agriculture activities. Google Earth Engine provides imagery datasets related to temperature, soil moisture, water history, and so on. In Google Earth Engine Sentinel-5P, NRTI O3 refers to the 'Near Real-Time Ozone dataset'. This dataset provides concentrations of Ozone (03) in the air; Ozone concentration in the air is one of the most reasons behind smog in summer.

Further, Sentinel-5P NRTI NO2 refers to the 'Near Real-Time Nitrogen Dioxide dataset'. It maps the layer of Nitrogen Dioxide on chosen land, further availability of Nitrogen Dioxide of chosen land can be calculated from the mapped layer. Sentinel-5P NRTI SO2 map near real-time Sulphur Dioxide concentrations layer on chosen land and Sentinel-5P NRTI CO map near real-time Carbon Monoxide concentrations layer on chosen land.

PDSI refers to the "University of Idaho Palmer Drought Severity Index" dataset, this dataset is a globally measurement of soil dryness based on temperature and recent precipitation. JRC Monthly Water History, v1.1 in GEE, is a global land water detection collection on month by month basic present since 1984. MOD11A1.006 refers to the "Terra Land Surface Temperature and Emissivity Daily Global 1km dataset", this dataset emissivity and daily land surface temperature globally. In this proposed research study, based on factors and by considering the importance of agriculture for the economy, an intelligent land suitability model will be constructed economically through an analysis of Google Earth Engine geo-environmental remote sensing datasets by utilizing machine learning techniques. The land suitability detection process will also help the future atmosphere and rainfall situation of the under-considered area to be identified and considered. Based on the factor discussed above, land suitability will be detected through the intelligent model economically. Many factors will be considered behind land suitability detection, such as whether the land has enough soil nutrition, land-water history, climate, and rainfall situation.

The land suitability detection model will be constructed through an analysis of different imagery geo-environmental time-series datasets, e.g., "Terra Land Surface Temperature and Emissivity Daily Global 1km dataset", "Near Real-Time Nitrogen Dioxide dataset", "University of Idaho Palmer Drought Severity Index", " JRC Monthly Water History, v1.1" available on Google Earth Engine data catalog. Further different machine learning techniques will be used behind the analysis of the above-mentioned geo-environmental datasets.

This research study will specifically focus on the agriculture land of Pakistan, due to the large cultivation land availability and one of the large agricultural countries, among others. The purpose of this research study is to build an intelligent machine learning-based model which detects whether under consideration land is suitable for agriculture activities, a decision will be based on soil nutrition, moisture, water history, and surrounding air quality.

1.2 Google Earth Engine

Google Earth Engine provides a parallel high-performance computation service and holds analysis-ready multi-category geospatial datasets in petabytes. Google Earth Engine provides parallel data computation services, visualization of datasets in petabytes volume, and web-based applications prototype development. These services can be controlled and accessed through Google Earth Engine's own web-based interactive, integrated development environment programming interface (IDE), or GEE supported application programming interface (API). Google Earth Engine data catalog holds large publicly available geospatial datasets. These datasets are observations of different imaging systems in both non-optical and optical wavelengths and different satellite, land cover, socio-economic, topographic, environmental variables, weather, and climate forecast. GEE platform provides data in a preprocessed form and removes the issues associated with data management with the easy-access facility. Further, the user can either access the publicly available geospatial data on Google Earth Engine code editor and can easily analyze the data or can also import private data through the utilization of different GEE API libraries.

Google Earth Engine requires an account on its platform before accessing datasets, access to GEE code editor for data analysis, training videos, educational curricula, tutorials, code samples, user's guide, and data mining algorithms documentation. Any person having a GMAIL account can easily create an account on the Google Earth Engine platform by clicking on this URL https://signup.earthengine.google.com/. Google Earth Engine platform oriented towards novice users, but having prior experience in writing scripts, knowledge of GIS platform, and remote sensing knowledge is a great edge. It will help in enhancing and shaping skills of extracting useful and advance information from geospatial datasets.

Google Earth Engine data catalog holds a huge amount of data in petabytes, which are earth observations of satellite and remote sensing imagery of the earth. GEE data catalogue contains Landsat imagery, data of climate forecasts, socio-economic, geophysical, environmental, land cover data, forestry data, snow cover data, and imagery data from Sentinel-1 and Sentinel-2 satellite, and many other kinds of geospatial data.

1.3 Google Earth Engine Code Editor

GEE has the so named Software Editor an Integrated Design Area (IDE). The Program Editor has several functions in this setting that promote programming. Enter the following URL in your browser if you wish to use the download editor: https:/code.earthengine.google.com, A programming interface such as the one below, will appear. Figure 1 comments below refer to other functions. This window is used to type javascript code. The publisher also has several support features, such as autocompletion for Earth Engine tasks, and autocompletion of parentheses.

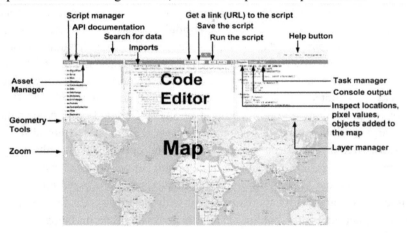

Figure 1 Google Earth Engine Code Editor

1.4 GEPHI

Gephi program is used for visualization of Google Earth Engine data sets. Gephi is an open-source visualization and network monitoring program. It uses a 3D rendering engine for real-time display of large networks and speeding discovery. A versatile, multi-task design brings new ways of working with complex data sets and generating useful visual outputs. It provides easy and broad access to data from the network and enables spatialization, inspection, routing, manipulation, and clustering. It can handle large networks (i.e. over 20,000 nodes), and it takes advantage of multi-core processors

14

because it is based on a multitasking model. Node architecture can be personalized; it can be a layer, a panel, or a picture rather than a traditional form. Highly configurable algorithms for the architecture can be tested on the graph window in real-time.

1.5 Pixel Based Classification

Throughout the pixel analysis, the spectral knowledge they provide is used to classify specific image pixels (Richards 1993). The pixels are the basic (spatial) unit in a satellite image. They also come automatically and therefore, can effectively be applied. It is the standard approach to classification. For pixel-based sorting, different systems are in operation. There are three of these: Total, max distance and max mahala Nobis reach. One believes that the groups have been defined objectively and that their measures and variances are known, for example. These three programs use a certain notion of 'width' to the class mean to determine which class pixels to allocate. The classifiers based on pixels only use the spectral signature for a specific pixel, and the classification of the entity often uses the spatial background of a pixel to support. Task Analyst provides many window form and size selection choices. A Manhattan (diamond) type with a width of 13 pixels was chosen for this classification. All feature classes were fitted with a minimum mapping unit (MMU) of 352 pixels (about 0.04 acres). Every specific class of features was categorized using the training collection. Therefore, all different functional groups provided a "wall-to-wall" grouping (Weih and Riggan, 2010).

1.6 Geospatial Data Analysis in Google Earth Engine

One of the most critical problems confronting us today is how to manage, interpret, and model details whether they are too many or too little. There are big challenges in working with broad or lengthy datasets, such as pattern identification, geophysical tracking, unusual occurrence detection (natural dangers), etc. There are often small complications. There, the key issues are how the seas of accessible knowledge are accessed, interpreted, and visualized. Machine Learning (ML) also involves the various architectural artificial neural networks (ANN) and support vector machines (SVM). It is a highly valuable tool for insightful study, manipulation, and simulation of geo- and environmental details.

1.7 Different Machine Learning Algorithm use for Analysis

Machines Learning (ML) is a mathematical and empirical analysis of algorithms for the effective accomplishment of a given function without the use of specific instructions, deduction, and computer machine trends. Artificial Intelligence (AI) sub-set is machine learning (ML). The ML generates a statistical model to execute the function and render projections or assumptions without the reference variables such as training data being directly coded.

1.7.1 Random Forest Algorithm

The class of all methodologies specifically built for decision tree is the Random Forests Classifier. It generates a large number of decision-making tree dependent on random data and a random variable preference.

1.7.2 Minimum Distance Algorithm

One of the easiest and most popular classifiers, the Minimum Distance Classifier still has success compared with the more complicated classifiers in literature. The center of this distinction relies on how different or close the evaluation examples are, and the teaching examples are from each other. Diff between the evaluation sample and the training data samples is defined by different steps in the minimal distance classification. Distance measurements, therefore, play a significant role in deciding the final classification efficiency. The most commonly used distance metric in the minimum distance classification is Euclidean distance.

1.7.3 Naïve Bayes Algorithm

For classification, Naive Bayes requires broad sets of training details. It means that a certain function exists independently of certain characteristics. Models and projections can be easily made.

1.7.4 CART Algorithm

A Decision tree algorithm that divides data into standardized subsets by using binary recursive partitions is the CART (classification and regression stack). The most discriminatory variable is chosen first as the root node in the branch node for the division of the results. The partitioning shall be replicated until the nodes are appropriately homogeneous. The terminal nodes (called leaves) represent class labels and branches in a tree structure represent conjunctions of features that lead to these class labels (Kotsiantis, 2013).

1.7.5 Support Vector Machine Algorithm

The Vector Machine Service (SVM) is an algorithm that can be used for classification or regression. It is often seen through problems of grouping. Throughout the SVM algorithm, each data object is drawn as a point inside an n-dimensional space (where n is the number of characteristics you have) with each attribute as its name. We then define the aircraft, which differentiates very well between the two groups.

1.8 Problem Statement

The development and growth of plants and crops heavily depend on the number of mineral nutrients and their concentrations available in the soil. Plants or crops sometimes face challenges in obtaining a sufficient amount of nutrients for the necessary cellular process from the soil due to immobility. The decrease in crop growth, fertility, or poor food quality happens due to deficiency of natural nutrients, sufficient water, soil moisture, and atmosphere quality requires to meet the demand of plants' necessary cellular process. Soil quality is an essential factor in agriculture, and mineral nutrients are usually obtained from soil; some plants cannot absorb nutrients from the soil due to the composition and chemistry of soil and hence result in lower production. In this research study, by considering above mentioned facts intelligent agriculture land detection or evaluation model will be constructed through an analysis of geo-environmental time-series imagery data available in Google Earth Engine by utilization of machine learning techniques to detect whether under consideration land is suitable for agriculture activities or not an economical way.

1.9 Research Questions

The following are the research questions:
- How does the proposed model facilitate farmers in assessing land quality for agriculture activities in an efficient way?
- What is the impact of the modern proposed land evaluation model on traditional land evaluation techniques, and how will the proposed model contribute to the economic boost?
- How will visualization of rainfall situation, temperature & emissivity, water history, and vegetation conditions in investigated land help farmers enhancing the healthy growth of crops?

1.10 Objectives

There are some specific objectives of this research as follows:
- To explore an analysis of Google Earth Engine global geo-environmental datasets for the rise of the agriculture sector and food production in Pakistan
- To Economically develop the land suitability detection model for agriculture activities
- To detect earlier land suitability for the management to make an informed decision that can boost the economy
- To identify or examine Pakistan's future atmosphere and rainfall situation in favour of further production and crop growth

- To create a facility for agriculture or environmental sector to take necessary actions earlier for better and more future production of crops, fruits, and vegetables in Pakistan
- To integrate machine learning algorithms for the detection of land suitability with old-school farming methods

1.11 Organizational Paragraph

This book rest organization is described as follows: Chapter 1 is the introduction of the A Smart Agriculture Land Suitability Detection Model Using Machine Learning with Google Earth Engine with 11 sections and 5 subsections. Chapter 2 has a literature review of this research with 1 section. Chapter 3 has the methodology and data collection of this research; in this chapter, we have the 13 sections. Chapter 4 has the results and discussion of this research; in this chapter, we have 8 sections. Chapter 5 has a conclusion and future work of the book; in this chapter, we have 2 sections.

2 Literature Review

2.1 Background Study

Many studies have been conducted previously on the detection of land suitability for agriculture. Some of these studies involve the collection of land samples from the actual field. Most of them involve human manual input for the decision about land suitability. Most of the studies involve old farming techniques for the detection of land suitability. In this paper, agricultural land suitability was evaluated through geographic information systems known as GIS designed to manipulate geographic data (Zolekar and Bhagat, 2015). In this research paper, a web-based framework was developed which gather various global online data and apply GIS techniques to detect land suitability for agriculture (Yalew et al., 2016a). In this research paper, an agriculture suitability detection map was developed by applying GIS and weighted overlay techniques with the integration of experts' opinions, literature review, and correlation techniques (Zolekar, 2018). In this research paper, the authors considered the natural capacity of the land unit and included environmental impact for agriculture land suitability detection; a GIS methodology and hybrid analytic hierarchy process was used to evaluate land suitability (Memarbashi et al., 2017). In this research paper, fourteen criteria were selected through the study of literature review and expert opinion for land suitability detection. Further GIS-based Analytical Hierarchy Process (AHP) was used to evaluate land suitability (Ahmed et al., 2016).

Another factor behind the limited productivity of agriculture is degradation and soil sealing; this paper focuses on determining actual degradation status in the concerned area through the utilization of geographic information system techniques. Another factor of land degradation is soil sealing, and fuzzy models were established to calculate land cover changes. The reason behind land degradation is over-irrigation, human intervention in the natural drainage process, and it produces inappropriate changes in agriculture practices (AbdelRahman et al., 2018). Soil type and soil-physicochemical characters such as organic matter, pH, EC, stoniness, derange, texture, depth, and slope are also essential factors behind identifying land suitability. In this paper, the suitability of investigated land was identified by applying the linear combination technique and analytical hierarchy process available in the GIS program on soil-physicochemical characters (Dengiz and Usul, 2018). Several new techniques and technologies are being implemented with time. In this paper, a sensor-driven recommendation model was presented for assessing land suitability; different sensors were deployed in agriculture land or farm, and then acquired sensed data was given to Multi-Layer Perceptron or neural networks for the construction of agriculture land recommendation model (Vincent et al., 2019). In this research study, suitability of land

19

for barley production in northwest Iran was assessed by utilizing MCDA techniques (Matter Elements and Analytic Hierarchy Process); this technique integrated with Analytic Hierarchy Process (AHP) and GIS as well (Seyedmohammadi et al., 2019). In this research paper, vegetation cover changes were mapped through the utilization of different statistical techniques, and Google Earth Engine satellite imagery datasets were used in this research study (Xie et al., 2019b).

The dry season in Northeast Thailand is where Cassava plants are cultivated, but most farmers do not know if that land is appropriate to grow Cassava plants because of minimal guidelines on agricultural planning. In this article, the writers suggested a statistical model of a machine-learning decision tree for land suitability in Northeast Thailand. Satellite images and land features were used (Mbugua and Suksa-ngiam, 2018) in this report. This paper blends professional structures and spatial IT capabilities to help develop a blueprint for land suitability. The consequence is the machine LEIGIS that permits analytical research in this article. The model used is based on the FAO land classification of crops and soil mechanic and environmental data defining an agricultural region. There are two aspects of the property evaluation: physical assessment and economic assessment. Data for 17 characteristic land characteristics were used for the physical assessment of the land, and a Boolean classification system was introduced. Models of general agriculture and five particular crops (wheat, barley, maize, cottonseed, beet sugar) are used.

The map values in terms of a land property are provided with a new interpolation function. The economic appraisal requires the maximization of wages in terms of business restrictions. To assist land evaluation and make improvements in its rules based on various accomplishments found in local communities, the expert framework has been created. The GIS features enable spatial data collection and performance analysis. The built framework allows it possible for all spatial datasets to be analyzed and displayed without needing any special programming skill (Kalogirou, 2002). The assessment of land suitability in water scarcities consists of an examination of land resources and the surface water capacity for various plant species to determine the need for additional river irrigation. Linguistic terminology may convey a vast volume of knowledge relevant to the suitability of plant property. For fuzzy rule-based structures, capacities of fuzzy sets for simulation containing ambiguity and vagueness are used where linguistic parameters for decision-making are represented as fuzzy laws. For this analysis, the Geographical Information System (GIS) framework establishes a fugitive rule-based inference method to determine land fitness for the specified crop, taking into consideration both land capacity and surface water potentiality. As several attributes are involved in decision-making, it is challenging to depict the attributes in a standard size, quantify the attributes, and build the rule-base. A new methodology is introduced in this review, in which attributes are listed systematically in separate groups to

20

approximate the intermediate suitability indices, to model the heterogeneous suitability parameters that include a wide number of attributes.

For calculating the aggregated impact of attributes within each category, the weighted linear agglomeration procedure and the yager aggregation approach are used and the results are compared. Also, the laws are based on the intermediate indexes for land suitability. The model was applied in West Bengal (India) to a submarine of the Gandheshwari region. ERDAS IP ver. 9.1 is used to construct the input attributes in the GIS raster-map format, and the output is created in the form of a thematic chart showing the appropriateness of a cell (20 m = 20 m) for the crop selected. The Yager aggregation approach in the case study region was considered more effective than the widely employed weighted linear aggregation system for land suitability assessment. 23% of established paddy fields, because of low surface water capacity and unsuitable terrain conditions in the zone, were found to become less suitable/unsuitable for paddy. The GIS approach is efficient in the management of vast volumes of knowledge on attributes and helps determine land suitability in farm watershed (Reshmidevi et al., 2009).

After the 1990s, land suitability evaluation in China has advanced quickly and played a central role in land use planning overall. The determination of land suitability for farming is constantly changing. Agricultural land suitability assessments for land conservation have been broadly applied in ecologically vulnerable areas, and individual crop assessments have increasingly grown. Surveys have also been common and effectively conducted for non-agricultural uses such as urban land use, tourism land use, farm acquisition, and other farm use. By widening the areas of assessment of suitability, new assessment criteria slowly come to light, and focus has been given to assessment considerations that have provided the outcomes from measurement perfections and not just human ones but also social, economic, and psychological ones. Thanks to the implementation of the philosophy of landscape ecology, the modern appraisal perspective was developed, and the concept of balanced land use was embraced and used in most evaluations. While standard techniques such as the weighted sum model, the linear regression and the research hierarchy (AHP) methodology is often used for land suitability tests, many strategies have been attempted to develop evaluation models, such as the Fuzzy mathematics model, the artificial neural grids (ANN) and genetic algorithms. A common GIS was used for land suitability assessment, and the introduction of assessment models in GIS has rendered the land adequacy assessment method more flexible (Shi et al., 2007).

Our study analyzed the optimum usage of land resources in Tabriz County, Iran, for agricultural growth. A judgment on GIS-based multi-criteria research was taken to determine land suitability. A variety of suitability criteria were assessed based on the experience of stakeholders, including climate, climatic conditions, and water quality at various stages. The different suitability considerations were determined by an objective hierarchical method and the weights culminated in the formation of the correct map layers. The weights extracted were used in this, and land suitability maps were subsequently produced for irrigated farming and dry farming. Finally, combining these maps and comparing the product with current SPOT 5 Satellite images produced a synthesized land suitability map. The suitability maps indicate growing areas will raise, decrease, or stay unchanged in the strength of soil usage for agriculture. In our research, 65676 hectares may be ideal for irrigation and 120872 hectares for dry-farm growing. It indicates a tremendous ability to satisfy the increasing regional market for agricultural products. Our work findings have been given and will be used in strategic land management (Feizizadeh and Blaschke, 2013) for the regional authorities. A significant and growing GIS function is the simulation of land suitability to help particular land uses. Three conventional models are analyzed in a simplified context, described by fluent logic theory, specifically bypass/fail screening, graded screening and weighted linear combination. The logic behind each prototype is clarified by the principles of fluid intersections, fluid unions, and fluid combining operations. Through these furious implementations of these three classic models, the distribution of kudzu in the conterminous USA is then operationalized and analyzed. The fuzzy models are more predictive than their classic counterparts. Such fuzzy models often generate more detailed fuzzy suitability maps by integrating environmental variables' fuzzy suitability into the modeling method. Such fuzzy maps may be converted into traditional maps with well-specified limits utilizing a defuzzification method, which is inappropriate for individuals to use with fuzzy results (Qiu et al., 2014). Boolean solutions to land appropriateness consider as specifically specified the geographical units and the meaning ranges. The continuing essence of land resources and the fluctuations and insecurities of calculation are neglected.

This article aimed to evaluate two approaches to assessments of land suitability; Parametric and Fuzzy multi-criteria methods to model olive growth opportunities in Libya's Jeffara Plain. A variety of parameters for soil and landscape were established in this paper, their weights were stated after consultations with local experts. The method of Fuzzy MCE is greater than that of parametric. The Soft MCE strategies tolerate the consistency of several soil characteristics and include more logical distributions of olive value for land suitability. Fuzzy MCE 's findings have shown that the majority of the region surveyed is extremely appropriate for olive production.

In contrast, findings deriving from the usage of the parametric test have shown that the majority of the field of study is moderately appropriate for olive production (Elaalem, 2013). Arable land resources are also being used, increasing tension between a growing populace and a decline in arable land supplies, leading to the rapid expansion in industrialization and urbanization in China. How arable land in the Qinghai Tibet

Plateau can be cultivated and abused has therefore attracted considerably more attention to the poor protective condition of arable land. Nevertheless, before developing and utilizing protected arable land, an acute assessment of natural suitability is needed.

As assessment factors, eight elements were taken from landform, climatic, soil, and water: slope, elevation, pitch direction, temperature, temperature, precipitation, depth of soil, organic matter content and water distance. The proof process's fugitive weight, guided by both information and facts, was used to achieve a natural suitability evaluation of arable land assets, compared with the findings measured with an applied index model. The results were measured. The assessment findings indicate that, based on a minimum of five suitability categories, 99.38% of the arable land 'references' is above the third category. That suggests a streaming proof weight model will accurately determine the inherent suitability of allocated arable land. Furthermore, 90.83% of arable land capital surpassed the third category, which suggests that the data's flouted weight is more impartial and rational than the full index model in this case, as opposed to the judgment's outcomes of a complete index model. So, it overcomes arbitrary arbitrariness of various human factors in deciding the weight and in measuring difficulty. Thirdly, the geological condition of 11 434,1 square kilometers of protected arable property, of which grades 1, 2, 3, 4 and 5 constitute 9,6%, 5,5%, 38,6%, 22,8% and 23,4% respectively. And we propose that the key areas for the potential creation of protected arable land should be Shigatse, Konggar, Chanang, Lhazê, Nêdong, Lhasa and Bainang counties (Jin et al., 2013).

Wheat is known as Egypt's most valuable grain, but not all Egyptian land is suitable equally to grow wheat. This analysis's key aim was to establish a spatial model for an evaluation of the suitability of wheat crops combined with GIS. Factors that affect the land's suitability for wheat crop have been described as organic matter, N, P, K, Zn, drainage, texture, density, topography, surface stoniness, hard saucepan hydraulic conductivity, water power, salinity, SPS, $CaCO_3$ and PH. Three thematic metrics were used to determine soil suitability, soil productivity, chemical, and health efficiency indices. The findings of the experiment were contrasted with the core and tale approaches of the Square root. About 29% of the region surveyed was moderately suitable and inappropriate for wheat production, and the areas related to the soil's adverse physical and chemical properties. By evaluating the outcomes of the three methods used, the existing model is strongly compatible with the Square root system, whereas all land units but one unit are in the same suitability level. The new model allows for findings that tend to suit actual conditions in the area (El Baroudy, 2016). The determination of land suitability (LSE) is an essential phase in the preparation of land usage. A versatile and efficient solution for this assessment process is the use of Multi-Criteria Decision Making (MCDM) technologies focused on regional information systems. Implementation of the MCDM Sensitivity Analysis will improve the interpretation of LSE findings and further guide planning decisions. A lack of visibility into the spatial measurements is the key drawback in sensitivity research in MCDM implementations. This paper proposes a new paradigm that includes details on spatial configuration from sensitivity analysis for MCDM to deal with this problem. The system comprises of an appraisal of land appropriateness and a spatially specific study of vulnerability. The sensitivity measurement incorporates spatial visualization and coordinated measures, including standard measurements and a modern and specific space measure (Earth Movers Distance EMD). The measurement of sensitivity involves the mean absolute shift rate MACR. A typical area was examined in the recently restored Yili zone of China. We thought the only cause of uncertainty was weights and a one-dimensional sensitivity model was used. This experiment showed that the LSE expert results are robust but relatively sensitive to weight changes in local areas. Our results suggest that the MACR and EMD will classify specific parameters effectively based on various sensitivity aspects. The EMD discusses the latest spatial element knowledge that is distinct from conventional sensitivity research approaches. This methodology offers an adequate basis for the efficient application of MCDM for reliable LSE tests focused on a spatially specific sensitivity study (Xu and Zhang, 2013). Changing natural conditions determine the suitability of the land for farming. Increase demand for fuel, fuel, fiber and bioenergy raises strain on the soil and brings in trade-offs between different land uses and resources to habitats. A stock of potentially suited areas for agriculture under increasing climatic conditions is therefore important. The 16 main food and energy crops are cultivated at a space-resolution of 30 Arc seconds dependent on the atmosphere, soil, and topography, utilizing a strange rational method to assess the global agricultural fitness. To evaluate their capacity for agriculture, we present our findings for current environment conditions (1981-2010) and consider irrigated areas in the present day and examine separately the appropriateness of heavily forested and protected regions. In comparison to the period between 2071–2100 and 1981–2010, the impact of climate change on agricultural adequacy in SRES A1B conditions, as simulated by the global climate model, ECHAM5, is shown. We also observed that climate changes would further extend suitable crops, particularly in high latitudes in the North (mainly in Canada, China and Russia), to 5.6 million square kilometers. The Global South, primarily in tropical areas, has the most vulnerable areas with the suitability, where even the suitability of multiple crops is reduced (Zabel et al., 2014). The development of Nicotiana tabacum L. is significant as more than 300 million smokers are still present in China. Because arable land is declining, it is essential to allocate tobacco to the most appropriate regions, precisely for the best yield. We thus determine the suitability of land for cigarette development in the Shandong province, China tobacco area. Twenty parameters, including climatic, soil and nutrient characteristics and topography details, were included in the evaluation. In order to construct land suitability charts, the fuzzy set-up, the analytic hierarchy method and the GIS methodology were combined. Tests showed that 29.82% of the overall region was extremely suitable and 17.74% unacceptable for tobacco development. Land in the west of the area became more suitable, while the east land around the yellow sea was less suitable. The number of days with a regular temperature of about 20°C and Mg with high soil exchangeable was the most restricting factor. This research reveals that Fuzzy Sets are an outstanding means of translating numerical details of various magnitudes into membership ratings that reflect land suitability. AHP is an effective and superior tool for routinely and objectively evaluating the weights of several variables. The simulation findings are focused on a specific land mapping framework, which includes the distribution and control of land properties. It has culminated ineffective strategies to increase the productivity of land use and better control of tobacco production (Zhang et al., 2015). One of the key triggers of deforestation and soil loss, which badly requires sensible land management policies, is agricultural activities. Agricultural activities. Land use planning is a conceptual activity which needs to estimate the eco-hydrological consequences of changes in watershed land use. The approach, based on a combination of land-use scenarios and simulations of hydrological models, typically guides land use and land management. Nevertheless, plans for land usage frequently neglect the clear environmental circumstances of the surrounding environment. In this paper a suitability evaluation method for obtaining land use plan scenarios was established, which took into synthesis the topographic, soil, environment and water supply circumstances of farmland upstream of the Huaihe basin. The SWAT model was used to test the impact of land-use situation impacts on eco-hydrological responses. The SWAT model was used in the future. In 2000, calibration and validation models based on land use status were performed, after which validated simulations based on scheduling scenarios were conducted. The results of the suitability assessment showed that 40.83% of existing farmland in 2000 was considered unacceptable, especially in the northern part of the studied region, where grass and forest plantations are carried out to extract short- and long-term land planning scenarios.

The SWAT model has been designed for the area studied with daily time. The combination of rainfall and runoff with the amount for calibration and testing period Nash – Sutcliffe (NSA) was accurately simulated. A temporal and spatial study was produced of relative shifts in eco-hydrological components represented by the testing SWAT model. The simulation findings calculated over a variety of time scales revealed that the average rainfall and overall water production and the total sediment costs were lowered. However, the evapotranspiration was increased, both short- and long-term land-use planning. The declining surface runoff and the increasing flood was much

25

larger than the increasing lateral flow for runoff components. Sub-base research found that there have been spatial variations in the simulated shifts in response to eco-hydrological adjustments, while the de-farming percentages in the sub shore areas have been strongly linked to the de-farming declines and the de-flush of water. The eco-hydrological reactions to plan long-term land use were overall deeper than to plan short-term land use. This research offers an overall system of assessment of the suitability to establish a land-usage planning scenario to resolve the failure of the conventional land-use scenario (Yu et al., 2018a). In the Middle East and North Africa (MENA), where biophysical environments are poorly suitable for agriculture, increasing demographics faced unbeatable challenges to agriculture in providing potential food stability. Iran has long been searching for self-sufficiency as a major agricultural nation in the MENA Area, but its potential for land and water supplies to achieve this goal is largely unknown. We assessed the Iranian country's capacity to grow sustainable crops based on terrain, topography and environment conditions utilizing very high-resolution spatial data sets. We graded Iran's crop suitability as (million ha): quite decent 0.4% (0.6), decent 2.2% (3.6), fair 7.9% (12.8), mediocre 11.4% (18.5), weak 6.3% (10.2), unacceptable 60.0% (97.4), out-of-area 11.9% (19.4). Including overall constraints induced by low precipitation, the primary soil and elevation influences restricting Iran's agricultural land included low organic material, steep slopes, and high ground sodium content. Approximately 50% of the croplands that occur in Iran are found in poor quality lands and are unsustainable. Cropland extension will not allow for the output increase, but redistribution into more appropriate areas will improve biodiversity and lower pressures on Iran's water supplies, land and ecosystems (Mesgaran et al., 2017). Land suitability analysis is a prerequisite for successful aquaculture and site selection both affects the development's success and durability. An appropriate approach is desperately required to enable site selection developers to establish aquaculture. The selection of the location can be viewed as a decision-making challenge with various parameters (MCDM). A documented, powerful approach used to tackle the issue of position selection is the application hierarchy procedure (AHP). This article applied the AHP system (GIS), and the MCDM to decide areas suitable on the coast of Hormozgan, Iran for shrimp aquaculture production. For the creation of templates, layer combinations were performed using the Boolean operators and the WLC process. The findings are described and evaluated after running the mixture models. Evidence evaluation indicates that several of the acceptable areas in the WLC model complement the present shrimp facilities, suggesting the usefulness of the WLC concept based on the GIS. Throughout the eastern portion of the research, regions are the regions with the strongest targets. Since current shrimp farms cover a limited part of the research, it is necessary to extend shrimp agriculture further in other areas (Hadipour et al., 2015). The land suitability assessment may be automated via artificial intelligence and machine learning approaches. Multiple MCS or ensemble methods expand quickly and attract much scrutiny, and in many cases, they have proved more accurate and reliable than an outstanding single classification scheme. A land suitability classification based on the dataset is analyzed in this report. The recently developed RotBoost-generated ensemble classification methodology is used to create a hybrid of Rotation Forest and AdaBoost, and the first implementation for a suitability classification is known as RotBoost. The studies carried out on the Shaver plain field of northern Khuzestan, southwestern Iran. The tests are performed. In conjunction with the FAO process, the suitability groups for the input data is determined. It offers promising proof of the usage of machine learning approaches, in particular MCS methods in land suitability classification. The findings reveal that Rotation Forest or AdaBoost, which stands at around 99% and 88.5% may generate ensemble classifiers that have a far higher predictive accuracy than two separate performance appraisal measures (Mokarram et al., 2015).

However, land adequacy evaluation is always scarce in semi-arid areas of Iran for growing development and preparing a viable agricultural program. Therefore, we plan to determine land fits for two primary crops (i.e., rain-fed wheat and barley) based on the 'climate suitability evaluation process' of the Food and Agriculture Organization (FAO) for 65 km2 of farmland in the province of Kurdistan, Iran. Soil samples have been obtained from 100 layers of genomic soil profiles, and soil samples have been tested for physical and chemical properties. Also reported were topography and climate records. Following the estimation of land suitability groups for the two crops, machine learning (ML) and conventional methods were used to map them. There were major variations in the maps expected for both strategies. For example, the findings showed that the ML-based Land Suitability maps were more reliable than those of conventional approaches concerning rain-feed wheat. It was noted that areas with classes of N2 (Total 18%) and S3 (Total 28%) were larger and class N1 (Total 24%) area was less predicted in the traditional approach compared with the ML approach. The study also found that class N2 (Total 24%) was higher. The research area's main drawbacks were flowering snow, extreme hills, poor soil density, strong pH, and heavy gravel. Therefore, land management programs are planned to maximize productivity and establish a productive agriculture environment (Taghizadeh-Mehrjardi et al., 2020).

In planning and maintaining sustainable land usage, land suitability classification is relevant. Many land suitability research methods are time-intensive and costly, integrating a wide range of ground- and soil criteria. For this research, an efficiency-enhancing land suitability review was faced with a possible useful methodology (combined role selection and fuzzy-aHP method). For this, the three most productive land suitability criteria for the cultivation of just the Shaver Plain, southwest Iran, were calculated with three separate algorithms Random Scanning, Optimal Quest, and

Genetically Methods. Next, land appropriateness groups have been determined using the ambiguous AHP methodology for both processes. A random scan tool has been used to choose salinity (electrical conductivity (EC), alkalinity (EXP), sodium wetness and soil texture. The latest screening tool and genetic approaches have been used to find gypsum, EC, ESP and soil structure. The findings indicate that the traditional fuzzy-AHP models and procedures proposed in this analysis are widely accepted.

In contrast to the traditional fuzzy-AHP method, Kappa coefficient values were 0.82, 0.79 and 0.79 for the random quest, best quest, and genetic test. Our findings suggest that, following their respective weights derived from fuzzy-AHP, EC, ESP, soil texture and humidity may be better adapted for assessing the land suitability classification for the barely studied region's culture. Therefore, the combined function collection and the blurry AHP method will save resources and time to classify land suitability (Hamzeh et al., 2016).

For environmental modeling, risk analysis and decision making, reliable and precise spatial soil knowledge is important. Reload sensing results are found to be inexpensive and time-consuming as secondary sources of data in digital soil mapping in contrast with conventional approaches to soil mapping. Nevertheless, there has not yet been a complete analysis of remote sensing data's ability to boost knowledge on local soil scale in West Africa. The analysis work studied the spatial distribution of six soil properties sand, silt, sound, cation exchange power (CEC) and soil organic carbon (SOC) and spring of nitrogen in a 580 sq. Km agricultural watershed in Southwestern Burkina Faso, utilizing high-spatial-resolution satellite data (RapidEye and Landsat), land/climate data and laboratory analyzed soil samples. The findings of four computational predictive models were compared: Multiple linear regression (MLR), random forest regression (RFR), vector support (SVM). Cross-validation was carried out internally when estimates of individual samples from the simulation region and extrapolation field were confirmed. System efficiency stats show that computer instruction methods were slightly higher than the MLR, the RFR being the most effective in most situations. In the successful estimation of the soil properties in non-linear locations, MLR could not manage connections between dependent and independent variables. The most significant spectral predictors were considered to be satellite data obtained during the ploughing or early plant growth process (e.g., May, June), whereas the height, temperature, and predictive precipitation were prominent soil/climatic variables. The findings also revealed the influential predictors of optical land maps for the shortwave infrared and close in-frarouge Landsat 8 channels as well as soil-based indices of roughness, colour, and saturation. For more accessible data for Remote Sensing (e.g. Landsat, SRTM, Sentinels), the soil knowledge may boost comparatively low financial and workforce capacities at local and national scales in data-poor regions such as western Africa (Forkuor et al., 2017). The Multi-Criteria

Evaluation system (MCE) was implemented to generate optimal rural, environmental and urban environments. Two suitability maps have been optimized for SLEUTH's urban development model: agriculture and environmental conservation, while the suitability matrix for urbanization was used in evaluating results (Sakieh et al., 2015). This book gives a blueprint for assessing the suitability of the land in Azadshahr Township in north Iran for the cultivation of saffron (Crocus sativus L). The goal is to establish a specific methodological approach to assess land use's adequacy in Iran and other related regions for saffron cultivation (Maleki et al., 2017). This analysis aims to establish and test a land-appropriation model in the semi-arid area of North-Western Iran using topographical variables, soil data, and remote sensing data. A collection of 92 soil samples of agricultural land usage from the depth from 0 to 30 cm have been collected for this reason as a random stratified study (Ostovari et al., 2019). The goal was to decide different land suitability groups for the cultivation of saffron using AHP and GIS. A decision tree with physical, economic, and social criteria was created. We have used secondary data from accessible sources (meteorological evidence, remote sensing), and relevant primary data from the soil survey, interviewing's and expert opinions (Wali et al., 2016). For a supplement, the nodes on the network, a newly designed series of adaptability functions were used. Instead, ALECA was adapted to Central America and checked. The findings indicate that ALECA reliably assesses the suitability of real coffee areas for coffee output to be higher than non-coffee regions, even without the use of the coffee maps as a guide, and can accurately forecast the defined quality order for coffee reference zones in Central America (Estrada et al., 2017). Assessment of land suitability may help determine agricultural production growth strategies. AHP has been used to determine land suitability for agriculture development in hilly areas by incorporating GIS-based multi-criterion decision-making, utilizing DEM and Landsat 8 satellite data (Pramanik, 2016). This aims to apply the Logic Scoring of Preference (GIS-based LSP) methodology to evaluate agriculture-appropriate fields as an enhanced tool for making multicriteria decisions. The geological, topographic, landscape, environmental, land use, and accessibility requirements for the assessment were included (Montgomery et al., 2016). The research would evaluate three separate techniques against two strategies for suitability review. The primary approach will use the Analytical Hierarchy (AHP) Technique, while the second approach would use two methods: Fuzzy AHP and Nested Fuzzy AHP.

Secondly, each strategy should be tested to consider and demonstrate the role of complexity in model design and structure (Nguyen et al., 2015) in climate change scenarios. The second approach would use Fuzzy AHP. This research was undertaken to determine the suitability of land usage in the northeast of Iranian province Golestan for rainfed farming using the Geographical Information System (GIS). Next, numerous environmental variables were thematically described, including weather, atmosphere, and topographical variables (Kazemi and Akinci, 2018). Around the same time, this research explores the correct farmland and water supplies to optimize crop trends in the Shahreh Plain in the province of Chaharmahal-Va-Bakhtiari, Iran. 120 pedons, at an estimated 750 m radius, have been excavated, according to a semi-detailed soil survey. 19 pedons are deemed representative based on the pedons (Mosleh et al., 2017).

A crop suitability map showing areas suitable for farming activities in Taita Hills in Kenya will be extrapolated and produced by this analysis. It uses details on the environmental situation, height, precipitation, and other related case study parameters where variation in precipitation and repeated droughts significantly impacts people whose lives are primarily influenced by subsistence farming (Mundia, 2015). Throughout this context, the writers aim to chart the adequacy of agricultural land and define marginal land distribution throughout Malawi. Quantitative results were given for eight soil- and field factors and a spatial distribution map of land suitability was established using five separate models (Li et al., 2017). It tested the suitability for three attractive bio feed crops: switchgrass, miscanthus, and hybrid poplar, on the marginal lands of the Upper Mississippi River Basin (UMRB). Land suitability has been graded according to a whirlwind of reasoning dependent land suitability assessment procedure (Feng et al., 2017) in five grades of suitability (not, bad, center, decent, and extremely suitable). The purpose of this research is to evaluate the viability of picking, ranking, and weight variables quantitatively in the MCE utilizing empirical evidence of a sample area (Fu et al., 2018). This research proposed a recovery strategy that included land suitability analysis and evaluation of ecosystem resources for a mining site in the Chinese province of Liaoning. When evaluating their suitability rates, we measured land suitability for three restoration alternatives and identified appropriate land uses for each location (Wang et al., 2017). Soil and topography knowledge has been turned into blurry details for the application of climate data on land suitability. Following the assessment, the AHP (analytic hierarchy process) and the flourishing set approaches in ArcGIS setting were established to accurately assess land adequacy for wheat and maize farming (Pilevar et al., 2020). This solution will help land users or planners to evaluate their land more effectively and effectively. A Rules-Based System (RBS) algorithm is used to construct a structure into a series of rules that bind each other, leading to a conclusion of adequacy. There are other factors in the laws themselves, including annual precipitation, high altitude, rainfall, a form of soil, pH, the chance of floods, soil quality, solarium depth of soil and so on (Rahim et al., 2019).

Crop models have now been developed to produce strategic significance for country precision farm management. This analysis aims to produce the WHI via the hybrid method, which involves qualitative and quantitative factors such as expert and theoretical experience weighed by the analytical hierarchy (AHP) mechanism. This method has been incorporated into the analysis based on a Technique linear mixture.

30

The research field of wheat growing was performed in the Sogulca Basin on the Central of Anatolia province of Turkey, with a field of 68,04 km2. In the Basin, which is divided into 47 ground units in keeping with the thematic land diagram, we have chosen 10 parameters, both human, chemical, and topographical. 32.05% of the study area has been classified as highly and moderately suitable with the WSI model, while 67.95% of the total study zone has marginal properties for wheat cultivation, which are not appropriate. Results reveal that soil density, shape, and slope indicators were considered the most powerful markers of WSI's last score values. The WSI values for the model's testing were compared to five years (2013–2017) of yields and NDVI values, with a land rating for wheat being highly precise for yield r2 = 0.83% and NDVI r2 = 0.78%. The findings revealed that in semi-arid environments, the WSI was considered to be a comfortable pattern. Nonetheless, to be used as a general transfer index, we recommend that the WSI model be evaluated in a comparable climatic setting and various soils. Furthermore, we can integrate heterogeneous data to determine and classify suitable in agriculture, using AHP with GIS capability (Dedeoğlu and Dengiz, 2019). This research aimed to create a reconstruction model of adequacy evaluation in north-east Iran's western Mashhad suburbs. The redevelopment model helps to make cleaning place and healthy surroundings in urban municipalities and environmental agencies. A space-building technique has been used to evaluate ten appropriate spatial variables, including heights, dimension, geographical units, soil units, soil coverings, green capital, runoff, path proximity, and proximity to wells, utilizing the fuzzy logic and GIS methodology. In this sense. A final map of land suitability evaluation was produced by combining layers using standardized fuzzy GIS membership functions (Bikdeli, 2019).

In some fraudulent web sites that look like a real web page, we gain confidential details from the customer and carry out some illegal operation called phishing on the cyber globe. This phishing or deception method may be used by an intruder utilizing certain websites, which presents a significant danger for web users to their personal and sensitive details. This act is also a danger to all consumers of web sites in the area of e-banking and e-commerce. In this post, the diverse features of legal, suspect, and phishing websites are discernible. These features are fed to the built-in WEKA machine learning algorithms for comparison and accuracy testing. J48, Naïve Bayes, Random Forest, and Logistic Tree (LMT) are used in this analysis, measured correctly to determine the location's validity. The right algorithm may even be chosen between various algorithms. In this article, the findings are contrasted in two respects. We find the best algorithm by evaluating the numerous properties, such as the right classified instances, wrongly classified instances, mean absolute error, and kappa statistics. Second, these algorithms' precision is evaluated in the bar chart with various parameters such as TP rate, FP rate, Precision, Recall, F-Measure, the MCC, the ROC

Region, and the PRC Field. The chosen algorithm automates the method of website review. This prediction model may be used to assess this website's validity before making purchases on every e-commerce website (Latif et al., 2019b).

The patient is wearing a pulse monitor device and controls. Doctors are alerted by utilizing particular equipment, whether the patient's pulse is out of control with strict heart rate monitoring limitations, which is vital for cardiac patients since it indicates that every condition is detectable. Electrocardiography (ECG) is used to track heartbeat, but the (ECG) electrocardiography unit is in an uncommon shape. A way of measuring cardiac beat may be a pulse tracker, which can be of various sizes and shapes to determine the cardiac rhythm, and most of them of smart belts, smartphones, etc. Specifies that the heart stretches and contracts. The suggestion is that you can use the unique bracelet type system to monitor your pulse and then add data to the database to hold the records of the user. A registry is accessible for all patients for side-by-side medical background reports. The device has greater stability, performance and specificity for heartbeat tracking. Medical records would still be accessible to the practitioner. The doctor would also prescribe medicine. They are using machine learning methods and strategies for data processing and regression for a standard method using. The Circos method is used to display the output of the dataset. Linear regression (LM) algorithm and Classification and Regression Tree (CART) algorithm used for pulse measurement and heart rate prediction in R-language. In the end, IoT blends software and hardware to generate trillions of knowledge through connecting various techniques and sensors to the cloud and by utilizing innovative methods to make sense of data and knowledge (Tariq et al., 2019).

Millions of software are submitted every day by the users. Millions of people launch this software without testing and managing. These duplicate apps destroy the users ' trust in Google Play Store and enable them to capture sensitive user details. No more detail about the front end of the application is given by developers and will determine the application's validity. This article creates a Google Play Store list of all game types by using a Google Play Scraper. Cumulatively scrap the 3600 paying applications and 10k free software from all sports types, including at least 550 free and paid applications for each group by utilizing Google Play scraper. The implementations of these games are Term, Quiz, Gameplay, Sport, Tactics, Driving, Role Playing, Puzzle, Music, Educational, Deck, Casino, Casual, Screen, Adventure, and Arcade, respectively. Scrape a maximum of 70 attributes for each Google Playing Store programmed, but use four evaluated attributes in this paper: Downloads, Ads, InApplicationPurcahses and Scores, etc. In this article, you can see the InAppPurchasing levels of free and paid apps, the percentage of promotional funding required for free and paid apps, the free and paid application scores using histogram, free and paid application installations with a histogram of all game forms. Also, imagine the interaction between attributes in

CIRCOS. This simulation is particularly useful for software creators in the production process, and app players who want to play the game (Latif et al., 2019a).

Nothing may negate the value of interactive analytics. For the writer, it was still a matter of how to work with complex diagrams. Digital graphical processing is one of the main reasons for its exceptional and distinct presence in the world with data science. The study of graphs and large data also interested numerous scholars and scientists from around the world. The analytics will contribute to more valuable and efficient results in different domains like life sciences, industry, computer sciences, technology, and so on utilizing the most sophisticated tools for the graph. If introduced to graph analytical devices, biological data can be interpreted in an interpretable manner, which can contribute to useful insights. This article is meant to illustrate the graph using two separate methods. Diverse techniques such as the compilation of databases from heterogeneous biological data sources, data aggregation, and new system creation (MYBIOGRID) were used throughout this inquiry. Designing requests in Neo4j to visualize MYBIOGRID and to create a relationship using the property graph model using the Cypher Query Language. In the next stage, the data is submitted to CIRCOS, and motive similarity is visualized. The consequence of this analysis demonstrates that visualizing the similarity matrix of repeated patterns reflects the most related patterns in the series. Graphical databases play a critical function in graph analytics, but in-memory storage processing requires some time to process a large number of data sets. Every method has its basic parameters, making it a strong analytical and comparative choice (Tallat et al., 2019).

In the mobile device industry, the competitive advantage is preserved, and the requirements of the premium product are analyzed. In the smartphone app production sector, the customer input on these apps plays a crucial function. The rapid growth of web technologies enabled people to connect and convey their opinions on apps, to rank and share. This document has scrapped 506259 Google Play Store consumer feedback and applications in 14 separate groups. Different standard machine learning algorithms, such as logistic regression, the Random Forest Classification, and Multinomial Naïve Bayes, were used to calculate statistic details. To test Bigram, Trigram, and N-gram, different parameters, including accuracy, reminder, and F1 score were used, and the statistical outcome of these algorithms was compared. Machine Learning algorithms like Logistic regression, Random Forest, and Naïve Bayes, is tested, one by one, and the outcome evaluated. Logistic regression is assumed as the optimal method for Google Play Store research applications. The findings were statistically tested, and it was noticed that the practical regression method was correct to evaluate various responses based on three classes: optimistic, negative and neutral (Aldabbas et al., 2020).

The prediction of frost includes dynamic decision-taking using circumstances. Due to frost events, crop and flower output is decreased, and to mitigate the impact, we need to predict this occurrence. If the effects of the frost forecast are correct so that frost damage may be minimized. A community learning strategy is used in this paper for detecting frost events via the Convolution Neural Network (CNN). We have used this to obtain more effective and reliable performance. Frost incidents must be expected early, so that the farmer may take precautionary steps on time. For Google Play measurements and review, we scraped a data collection from various kinds of agriculture and gathered the top 550 agricultural applications of each category with 70 attributes for each group. Prediction of freeze incidents a few days before the real freeze occurrence with 98.86% precision (Latif et al., 2020).

Many injuries have been observed attributed to driver exhaustion. Drowsiness is a state of mind until the driver is unconscious, which ensures that the driver cannot adequately carry out his acts, like vehicle stopping and vehicle motion regulation. We developed an Array of stuff-based medical applications for driver drowsiness research. A design was suggested, and this scenario was tested in the NS3 WSN simulation platform. This analysis demonstrates that the injury level can be greatly decreased. When a driver's somnolence is detected, a warning alarm is sent to all vehicle drivers close to the sleeping driver, utilizing separate sensor nodes. The collective influence of sensor nodes is another special aspect of the sensor network mentioned here. A dataset in the medical apps field was scrapped for testing and evaluating Google Play software. The scraping was conducted with 550 applications of each medical field. Almost 70 attributes for each program in the Google Play store were scrapped for each group. In the future, wireless sensor networks are expected to be an interconnected part of our lives, rather than the existing personal computers (Ramzan et al., 2019).

The scope of secret practices utilized by communication networks has proved quite difficult to paralyzes their operations in the law justice community. To do so, criminal network analysis (CNA) tools must be given to law enforcement authorities and will offer sophisticated and detailed information for identifying the key participants (nodes) and connections (links) within the network. The creation of methods for predicting connections between participants relies primarily on models for social network analysis (SNA) and machine learning (ML) to boost model accuracy. The major challenge of creating classic ML models, including random forests with reasonable precision is collecting a sufficiently large dataset to train the model. The creation of a reasonably broad data collection for crime networks is a big challenge because of the extensive and secret existence of their operations about social networks. This research's main objective is to demonstrate that a prediction model based on a relatively limited dataset and data set produced by self-stimulation using DRL can lead to greater accuracy in predicting relationships. The model training was also paired with metadata (e.g.,

34

demographic characteristics such as criminal history, educational status, age, and proximity to the police station) to identify the real-life aspects of organized crime that would enhance model efficiency. Therefore a reference model without integrating metadata (CNA-DRL) has been compared to a model containing metadata (MCNA-DRL) to verify the findings (Lim et al., 2020).

In recent years, unmanned aerial vehicles (UAVs)/drones have been very common since they are used in many realms. They are commonly used in both civilian and military uses, including aerial imagery, television, missions for inquiry and rescue, identification, control of traffic, and logistics. Usually, the UAVs are used by various communication protocols such as MAV Link, Uranus Link, UAVCAN from a transmitter, or Ground Control Station (GCS). These communication protocols are used to share messages. The messages comprise essential UAV details and control commands sent from GCS to UAV or UAV to GCS. While these protocols offer improved connectivity together with safer features, most of these communications cannot be protected through a subtle method, and are vulnerable to many protection attacks such as the MITM assault, denial-of-services (DoS) assault, packet data injection attack, and eavesdropping. For instance, it may contribute to a military or civilian UAV crash land, steal substantial data from military activity, falsify information from surveillance or search and rescue mission, etc. There is also a need for a reliable communication protocol that will maintain the requisite UAV information protection standards collection. This study reveals implementations, general design, UAV attacks, and an overview of the protection problems of communication protocols with UAVs and provides a modern stable communication protocol for UAVs (Khan et al., 2020a).

Weather forecasting is a major environmental challenge which in the last century has appeared as one of the most challenging problems from a logical which innovative viewpoint. The authors analyse knowledge processing technology usage to calculate high temperature, precipitation, dissipation, and wind speed in this study. It was achieved with vector assistance profiles, decision tree, and weather details from 2015 and 2019 in Pakistan. A database framework for meteorological details was used for the preparation of workbook accounts. These estimates are addressed about normal implementation measures as well as the approximation that produced the best results for the generation of disposal rules for intermediate environmental variables. Similarly, a prophetic network model has been developed for the climate perspective programmed, contradictory results, and true climate information for the projected periods. The results show that data mining strategies can be used with sufficient case-specific information to estimate climate and environmental change (Saeed et al., 2020).

Data mining research has lately been based on data mining decision tree classification approaches, introducing a modern variable accuracy decision tree classification algorithm. The researcher uses the Rattle R and Weka data analysis method. Datasets for different age ranges are categorized by gender-based lung cancer care utilizing multiple types of treatment. The age range (30-60 years old) is both men and women with groups. The Decision Tree is an effective and optimal method for interpreting radiation and chemotherapy care outcomes within a particular age group community of Rattle R, and Weka tools determine the best method of treatment to evaluate the right treatment method. The forecasts are often contrasted with similar tables utilizing graph plots. This diagram corresponds with the projections. The investigator discusses the most effective and commonly employed methods of classification in the field of data mining and the core principles for the decision tree system. The two R and Weka data mining applications are mentioned briefly. This study's method was demonstrated by a comparison of 200 real data sets in terms of the accuracy of the classification among the two separate decision tree algorithms (Saeed et al., 2019).

Big data in the recent IT debate is a well-trafficked subject and does not neglect the existing study. In reality, the surplus resources relating to Big Data and how much of it are questionably accurate, due to the excellent work of experienced information marketing gurus, which can be challenging for a professional academic to handle at times. The Big Data and Network Intelligence Study Handbook on Patterns and Potential Guidance slices through shimmer and excitement around Large Data, offering a clear and convenient information tool of realistic academic usage. In this book, addressing subjects such as cloud computing, distributed computation, natural language processing, and customized well-being, we analyze current science, observations into recent trends, and literary limitations that suggest prospects for potential study (Zaman et al., 2015).

3 Methodology and Google Earth Engine Data Catalog

3.1 Introduction

This paper is a descriptive study on the Google Earth Engine platform. It provides a brief description of different geospatial datasets available in the Google Earth Engine data repository. Along with the description of other geospatial datasets, different societal issues are also mentioned, which can be resolved by utilizing geospatial datasets. Google Earth Engine platform provides several different machine learning or data mining algorithms for geospatial datasets analysis; a description of those algorithms is also provided in this research study. Datasets that are available in the Google Earth Engine catalog can be used to solve several social issues, and different scenarios are presented in this research study on an abstract level, which presented an idea that how we can utilize the Google Earth Engine platform and data mining for resolving the social issue. A different challenge that is faced by the Google Earth Engine platform such as scaling challenges, computational model mismatch, the client-server programming model is discussed at the end.

Google Earth Engine provides a parallel high-performance computation service and holds analysis-ready multi-category geospatial datasets in petabytes. Google Earth Engine provides parallel data computation services, visualization of datasets in petabytes volume, and web-based applications prototype development. These services can be controlled and accessed through Google Earth Engine's own web-based interactive, integrated development environment programming interface (IDE) or GEE supported application programming interface (API). Google Earth Engine data catalog holds large publicly available geospatial datasets, and these datasets are observations of different imaging systems in both non-optical and optical wavelengths and different satellites, land cover, socio-economic, topographic, environmental variables, weather, and climate forecast. GEE platform provides data in a preprocessed form and removes the issues associated with data management with the easy-access facility. Further, the user can either access the publicly available geospatial data on Google Earth Engine code editor and can quickly analyze the data or can also import private data through the utilization of different GEE API libraries.

Google Earth Engine requires an account on its platform before accessing datasets, access to GEE code editor for data analysis, training videos, educational curricula, tutorials, code samples, user's guide, and data mining algorithms documentation. Any person having a GMAIL account can quickly create an account on the Google Earth Engine platform by clicking on this URL https://signup.earthengine.google.com/. Google Earth Engine platform oriented towards novice users, but having prior experience in writing scripts, knowledge in the GIS platform, and knowledge about remote sensing is a significant edge. It will help in enhancing and shaping skills of extracting useful and advance information from geospatial datasets.

Google Earth Engine data catalogue holds a considerable amount of data in petabytes, which are earth observations of satellite and remote sensing imagery of the earth. GEE data catalogue contains Landsat imagery, data of climate forecasts, socio-economic, geophysical, environmental, land cover data, forestry data, snow cover data, and imagery data from Sentinel-1 and Sentinel-2 satellite and many other kinds of geospatial data. GEE platform provides the facility of uploading private data through the REST interface by using the command line or web-based tools, or users can request new additional data in the public data catalogue. Remote sensing earth imagery data in the public catalogue is continuously updating at the rate of 6000-scenes per day in case of active missions with a delay of 24 hours after scene acquisitions. Google Earth Engine uses a simple and 2D gridded raster bands data model with a lightweight container for images. Google Earth Engine imagery datasets contain a collection of images, and each image metadata consists of various information such as condition under images are collected, time, location, and images metadata associated with key/value. Images in remote sensory imagery data consist of multiple image bands, and each image band can be heterogeneous in projections or data types. However, pixels in bands need to be homogeneous in projections, resolution, and data types.

Google Earth Engine provides remote sensing imagery datasets in the preprocessed form, which facilitates the user in access and data analysis. GEE combined the related images in the form of the collection because a single sensor sense similar images, usually a collection of related images facilitates users in filtering data or selecting data that meets specific criteria, temporal or specific spatial. In Google Earth Engine, images are first to cut into tiles under images' original resolution and projection and then stored in a replicated and efficient tile database. Data ingestion in the form of tiles is a more efficient process than a traditional data cube system. This data ingestion concept usually reduces data degradation and preserve original image resolution, projection, and bit depth.

Google Earth Engine utilizes reduced resolution tiles pyramid concept, and reduced resolution tiles are created and stored in the tiles database. This process enabled improved and fast visualization of sensing imagery datasets at the algorithm development stage. The pyramid consists of multiple levels and each level of a pyramid created through the downsampling of the preceding level by a factor of two, and this process continues until the whole image fits into a single tile. The process of downsampling facilitates during the computation and analysis phase when a reduced resolution portion of the image is required at analysis; then, only the required tile is retrieved from the appropriate pyramid level. The concept of two-factor downsampling helps Google Earth Engine in providing preprocessed data at every scale without introducing storage overhead.

Google Earth Engine public data catalogue holds earth observation data, climate data, environmental data, air quality data, forestry data, socio-economic data and many more other kinds of data, these kinds of data can be utilized in resolving social issues of society or can be utilized in managing of future food need or in planning for preserving air quality for the future generation. Machine Learning or Data mining techniques are playing a significant role in the development of intelligent systems intended to use for smart city or social development. Google Earth Engine also provides great machine learning or data mining algorithms which can be used for the analysis of geospatial datasets, through analysis of geospatial datasets one can extract inside knowledge from massive data and can be utilized in the development of human society. The Following figure is a snapshot of Google Earth Engine code editor, a web-based integrated development environment (IDE) to analyze and visualize geospatial data. Google Earth Engine provides both supervised and unsupervised machine learning techniques for the analysis of data. In following Figure 2, on GEE code editor left-hand side pane, several supervised machine learning algorithms are given inside, "ee.Classifier" library tag. Some of these machines learning supervised algorithms are Cart, Decision Tree, Naïve Bayes, and SVM.

Figure 2 Google Earth Engine Code Editor and Machine Learning Classifiers

Unsupervised is also a machine learning or data mining technique which make cluster or group of data based on common characteristics exists within data. In Figure 3, on GEE code editor left-hand side pane, several unsupervised machine learning algorithms are given inside, "ee.Cluster" library tag. Unsupervised machine learning algorithms given in Google Earth Engine are CascadeKMeans, KMeans, XMeans, LVQ, and Cobweb.

Figure 3 Google Earth Engine Code Editor and Machine Learning Clustering Algorithms

In this research study, the Gephi program is used for visualization of Google Earth Engine datasets. Gephi is an open-source visualization and network monitoring program. It uses a 3D rendering engine for real-time display of large networks speeding discovery. A versatile, multi-task design brings new ways of working with complex datasets and generating useful visual outputs. It provides easy and broad access to data from the network and enables spatialization, inspection, routing, manipulation, and clustering. It can handle large networks (i.e., over 20,000 nodes), and it takes advantage of multi-core processors because it is based on a multitasking model. Node architecture can be personalized. It can be a layer, a panel, or a picture rather than a traditional form. Highly configurable algorithms for the architecture can be tested on the graph window in real-time.

This survey paper's primary purpose is to provide a brief description of geospatial datasets available on the Google Earth Engine platform with a thorough literature review and how we can utilize machine learning algorithms and geospatial data together for solving social issues. Recently and in the past, many researchers have utilized GIS techniques and specific geospatial data related to their problem of concern, and some have used machine learning techniques for resolving social issues. This research study's secondary purpose is to collect individual papers written on Google Earth Engine geospatial data analysis and construct a comprehensive survey paper. Papers were collected from Google Scholar based on a query of "Google Earth Engine data analysis," "Data mining on Google Earth Engine," "Machine Learning and geospatial data analysis," "Google Earth Engine datasets." The importance was given to those papers which were published within 10 to 15 years and related to Google Earth Engine.

The remaining structure of this paper is organized as follows. Section 2 consists of a description and literature study of various Google Earth Engine Data Catalogue datasets. Section 3 focuses on the Google Earth Engine frequently used algorithms. In section 4, the discussion revolved around geospatial data analysis and Google Earth Engine data analysis algorithms with their literature survey. Section 5 describes future work and several challenges which are faced by users while working on the Google Earth Engine platform.

3.2 Google Earth Engine Frequently Used Datasets

The most frequently used Google Earth Engine datasets are listed in the following Table 1. For the list of most frequently used datasets of Google Earth Engine platform, the necessary information was taken from this research article (Gorelick et al., 2017).

Table 1 Frequent Used Google Earth Engine Datasets

Dataset	Dataset Availability	Dataset Resolution	Dataset Coverage	Data Capture Period	Dataset Provider
GPWv4	2000–2020	30″	85°N–60°S	5 year	Center for International Earth Science Information Network
WorldPop	Multiple	100 m	2010–2015	5 year	WorldPop
ORNL DAYMET weather	1980–Now	1 km	North America	Annual	NASA ORNL
NEX downscaled climate projections	1950–2099	1 km	North America	1 day	NASA Earth Exchange
NCEP reanalysis	1948–Now	2.5°	Global	6 h	NOAA NWS National Centers for Environmental Prediction
CHIRPS precipitation	1981–Now	3′	50°N–50°S	5 day	University of California, Santa Barbara/CHG
GRIDMET	1979–Now	4 km	CONUS	1 day	University of Idaho
Global precipitation measurement	2014–Now	6′	Global	3 h	NASA PMM
NLDAS-2	1979–Now	7.5′	North America	1 h	NASA
NCEP climate forecast system	1979–Now	12′	Global	6 h	NOAA NWS National Centers for Environmental Prediction
TRMM 3B42 precipitation	1998–2015	15′	50°N–50°S	3 h	NASA GSFC
GLDAS-2	1948–2010	15′	Global	3 h	NASA
NCEP global forecast system	2015–Now	15′	Global	6 h	NOAA/ National Centers for Environmental Prediction/EMC

WorldClim	1960–1990	30″	Global	12 images	University of California, Berkeley
USGS National Landcover Database	1992–2011	30 m	CONUS	Non-periodic	United States Geological Survey
UMD global forest change	2000–2014	30 m	80°N–57°S	Annual	Hansen/UMD/Google/USGS/NASA
JRC global surface water	1984–2015	30 m	78°N–60°S	Monthly	Google/ European Commission JRC
GLCF tree cover	2000–2010	30 m	Global	5 year	NASA GLOBAL LAND COVER FACILITY
USDA NASS cropland data layer	1997–2015	30 m	CONUS	Annual	USDA National Agricultural Statistics Service
GlobCover	2009	300 m	90°N–65°S	Non-periodic	European Space Agency
PROBA-V top of canopy reflectance	2013–Now	100/300 m	Global	2 day	VITO/ European Space Agency
DMSP-OLS nighttime lights	1992–2013	1 km	Global	Annual	National Oceanic and Atmospheric Administration
USDA NAIP aerial imagery	2003–2015	1 m	CONUS	Sub-annual	United States Department of Agriculture Farm Service Agency
ETOPO1	Multiple	1′	Global	Single	National Oceanic and Atmospheric Administration
USGS GMTED2010	Multiple	7.5″	83°N–57°S	Single	United States Geological Survey
USGS National Elevation Dataset	Multiple	10 m	United States	Single	United States Geological Survey
EO-1 Hyperion hyperspectral radiance	2001–Now	30 m	Global	Targeted	United States Geological Survey
Shuttle Radar Topography Mission	2000	30 m	60°N–54°S	Single	Consultative Group for International Agricultural Research/NASA
GTOPO30	Multiple	30″	Global	Single	United States Geological Survey
L1 T radiance	2000–Now	15/30/90 m	Global	1 day	NASA LP DAAC at the USGS EROS Center
Global emissivity	2000–2010	100 m	Global	Once	NASA LP DAAC at the USGS EROS Center
MOD08 atmosphere	2000–Now	1°	Global	Daily	NASA Goddard Space Flight Center
MOD13 Vegetation indices	2000–Now	500/250 m	Global	16 day	NASA LP DAAC at the USGS EROS Center
MCD43 BRDF-adjusted reflectance	2000–Now	1000/500 m	Global	8 day/16 day	NASA LP DAAC at the USGS EROS Center
MOD44 veg. cover conversion	2000–Now	250 m	Global	Annual	NASA LP DAAC at the USGS EROS Center
MOD09 surface reflectance	2000–Now	500 m	Global	1 day/8 day	NASA LP DAAC at the USGS EROS Center

MOD10 snow cover	2000–Now	500 m	Global	1 day	National Snow & Ice Data Center
MCD12 Landcover	2000–Now	500 m	Global	Annual	NASA LP DAAC at the USGS EROS Center
MCD15 Leaf area index/FPAR	2000–Now	500 m	Global	4 day	NASA LP DAAC at the USGS EROS Center
MOD17 Gross primary productivity	2000–Now	500 m	Global	8 day	University of Montana Numerical Terradynamic Simulation Group (NTSG)
MCD45 thermal anomalies and fire	2000–Now	500 m	Global	30 day	NASA LP DAAC at the USGS EROS Center
MOD11 temperature and emissivity	2000–Now	1000 m	Global	1 day/8 day	NASA LP DAAC at the USGS EROS Center
MOD14 Thermal anomalies & fire	2000–Now	1000 m	Global	8 day	NASA LP DAAC at the USGS EROS Center
Sentinel 2A MSI	2015–Now	10/20 m	Global	10 day	European Union/ESA/Copernicus
Sentinel 1 A/B ground range detected	2014–Now	10 m	Global	6 day	European Space Agency
Landsat 8 OLI/TIRS	2013–Now	30 m	Global	16 day	NASA/ United States Geological Survey
Landsat 7 ETM+	2000–Now	30 m	Global	16 day	NASA/ United States Geological Survey
Landsat 5 TM	1984–2012	30 m	Global	16 day	NASA/ United States Geological Survey
Landsat 4–8 surface reflectance	1984–Now	30 m	Global	16 day	NASA/ United States Geological Survey

3.3   Google Earth Engine Data Catalog

Google Earth Engine online data repository holds more than 600 various kinds of geospatial datasets, and these datasets are up to 29 petabytes combined in size. Google Earth Engine data catalog size is three times bigger than all uploaded images in the first year of Google photos. Google Earth Engine data catalogue holds data of two distinct categories one is imagery collection data, and the other is vector data in the form of tables. Google Earth Engine data management team automatically maintained and updated datasets after every six hours or daily. Support of data management from Google Earth Engine provides user freedom to invest more time only in an analysis of data. Datasets classification of Google Earth Engine data catalogue. The data catalogue is divided into two different datasets categories one is vector datasets, and another category is image collection datasets. Vector datasets are in the form of tables and examples of vectors. These datasets are 'Protected Areas database,' 'US Census,' 'Eco

Regions', and 'International Boundaries.' The Second category of datasets available in the Google Earth Engine data catalogue is "Image Collection Datasets," these types of datasets consist of collecting remote sensing imagery or on earth observations imagery captured through different satellite. Examples of "Image Collection Datasets" are 'Geophysical datasets,' 'Climate and Weather Datasets,' and 'Imagery datasets.' Further sub-categories datasets of "Image Collection Datasets" are shown in Figure 4.

GOOGLE EARTH ENGINE DATASETS CLASSIFICATION

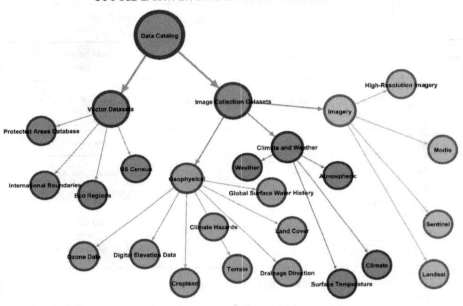

Figure 4 Google Earth Engine Datasets Classification

3.4   Vector Datasets

Vector datasets are those datasets that are in the form of tables. Each table has associated with a Unique table-Id. Users can utilize vector datasets in their code-scripts by mentioning the table-id of the required vector dataset. Google Earth Engine provides the facility of creating feature-based datasets to its users; for this purpose, the FeatureCollection method is used to combined multiple features about data into a single table form. For the creation of features-based data, the user has required to list down the features in the FeatureCollection constructor. FeatureCollection method facilitates users in sorting, rendering, and filtering of data. By mentioning the table-id of the required available vector dataset in the FeatureColection method, users can import

44

vector datasets into their code-scripts. Google Earth Engine vector datasets, as shown in the following Figure 5.

3.4.1 World Protected Areas

World Protected Areas dataset contains complete and most up to date information about protected areas of the world. This dataset is publicly available in Google Earth Engine in two different forms. One form is a polygon, and the other is form points. This dataset contains information about 200 thousand protected areas of the world.

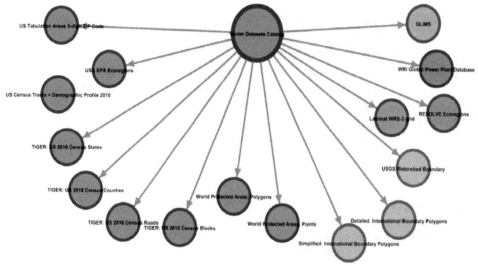

Figure 5 Google Earth Engine Vector Datasets

World Protected Areas (Points) dataset represents the center of the protected areas. This dataset provides by the UN Environment World Conservation Monitoring Centre (UNEP-WCMC)/ Protected Planet, and it is freely available in Google Earth Engine. A world protected areas database is used by different international bodies, scientists, NGOs, and private sectors tracking targets regarding the progress of protected areas and developing progress indicators. Protected areas database can be used to identify the most suitable areas for the establishment of new protected areas. This strategy will help achieve essential elements of the Aichi Biodiversity Target.

3.4.2 International Boundary Polygons

International Boundary Polygons dataset derived from two different datasets. One is the Large-Scale International Boundary (LSIB) file, and the other is World Vector

Shorelines (WVS) file. This dataset represents the interior and exterior boundaries of a country, data of exterior boundaries derived from the World Vector Shorelines file, and inner boundaries data consisting of sovereignty, boundary disputes, and boundaries policies by the U.S. government. Each feature of this dataset represents the country's disjoint area in the polygon area form, so considering the fact mentioned above, a country can consist of dataset multiple features.

Within the Google Earth Engine application collection, the regional boundary polygon dataset is included in two variants. Simplified: Large International Boundary Polygons, and Detailed: Large International Boundary Polygons, one edition. In a simplified version of the International Boundary Polygons dataset, smaller and medium islands are excluded, and some countries' disjoint regions are limited to only a single feature. In a detailed version, smaller and medium level islands are included. This dataset can help different local, regional divisions, financial institutions, and emergency response centers in the creation of interactive and user-centered applications. By utilizing international boundaries dataset, companies can track whether their self-driving cars are being compliant with national, local, or state laws or not. Further, local or regional disaster response centers can develop interactive mobile applications and improve their emergency response by utilizing International Boundary Polygons datasets in their system.

3.4.3 USGS Watershed Boundary Dataset

United States Geological Survey is a provider of USGS Watershed Boundary Dataset, and it is publicly available in the Google Earth Engine data catalogue. USGS Watershed Dataset provides an identification method and subdivides area of drainage. The Watershed boundary dataset provides the extent of all possible watersheds located on earth's surface, which leads the surface water towards major outlet points (e.g., stream, river). Earth's surface consists of a vast number of watersheds, and each watershed is identified through Hydrologic Units (HU) or Hydrologic codes. USGS Watershed Boundary dataset can be considered an essential tool that can be utilized to develop water resources management plan for local or even national level. Further, the USGS watershed boundary dataset provides the areal extent of the watershed, which could help farmers in the assessment of surface suitability before organizing agriculture activities. Watershed boundary data could also help farmers in identifying appropriate farming area near to suitable watershed.

3.4.4 Landsat WRS2 Grid Dataset

Landsat sensors are usually responsible for observing changes on earth and provides earth remote sensing imagery at spatial resolution. Usually, Landsat sensors record energies emitted from the earth's surface in various wavelengths of the electromagnetic spectrum. Emitted energy might be in the form of colossal radio waves, tiny gamma rays, and x-rays. The human eye is very sensitive and can only see reflected light, which lies between violet to red. Landsat 7 and Landsat 8 sensors usually record those lights which the human eye cannot perceive, such as thermal-infrared, mid-infrared, and near-infrared light and provides these data in digital form.

WRS stands for a worldwide reference system, the WRS dataset used as a global notion system for satellite data. Landsat sensors are continuously observing the earth and are recording emitted energies from the earth's surface worldwide since 1972. WRS system is proved to be especially useful in referencing satellite imagery, cataloging satellite imagery, and daily usage of satellite imagery. Landsat sensors or satellites are revolving around the earth into their orbits for capturing earth observations imagery, so each satellite image is associated with a path and row number. WRS data is a useful tool for identification of path and row of each satellite image, a descending orbit of a satellite referred to as path, and each path is subdivided into 119 rows started from north to south. A user can investigate about satellite image of any portion of the world by mentioning its path and row. Landsat 4, 5, and 7 use the WRS2 notion system, which is available in the Google Earth Engine data catalog in a manageable and preprocessed form. Landsat and Landsat WRS2 Grid datasets can be utilized in the assessment of change in land-use, the growth rate of population, movement of sea-ice, monitor water quality, the health of coral-reef, the encroachment of invasive species, and deforestation rates.

3.4.5 RESOLVE Ecoregions Dataset

The ecoregion is defined as a geographical area that has a particular type of natural features and natural environment; in other words, ecoregions are also defined as ecosystems of geographical area. Ecoregions are those geographical areas which consist of all taxa, including flora, these geographical areas are suitable for sustaining ecological process. Ecoregions are those geographical areas which consist of all taxa, including flora. These geographical areas are suitable for sustaining the ecological process. The ecological map or dataset was first constructed in 2001. It was introduced by NGO named RESOLVE Biodiversity and Wildlife Solutions and still has been used by different researchers, public or private organizations, and scientist communities. Earth is passing through many climatic and biodiversity changes each year; by considering these changes, an updated version of the Ecoregions map named RESOLVE Ecoregions was introduced in year 2017RESOLVE Ecoregions map or dataset is based on 846 terrestrial ecoregions of our living planet.

In the RESOLVE Ecoregions dataset, 846 terrestrial ecoregions are categorized into 8-realms and 14-biomes biogeographical divisions. Further subdivisions of biomes are made in which 8 are non-forest biomes, and the remaining 6 are forest biomes. Terrestrial ecoregions boundaries of forest regions and protected areas were intersected with another data named "Global Forest Change" of the year 2000 to 2015, this intersection helps percentage calculation of habitats living inside and outside of protected areas in the context of forest biomes. Same as protected areas and ecoregions, boundaries of non-forest areas were intersected with "Anthropogenic Biomes data," this intersection helps in calculation of remaining habitats percentage living inside and outside of protected areas. This dataset is derived from natural boundaries rather than political boundaries and can help support and monitor ecosystems and conservation planning and can help in the representation and management of earth biodiversity.

3.4.6 WRI Global Plant Database

WRI Global Plant Database holds power plants data collected from worldwide, this dataset is publicly available in the Google Earth Engine data catalog, and the World Resources Institute is the official provider of this dataset. This dataset was becoming publicly available in June 2018, and at that time, it contained information about 28,500 powerplants from around 164 countries. This dataset's purpose was to arrange globally powerplants information at a centralized database, which could help draw insights from data effectively. Entries of database consist of various information about powerplants such as geolocation, powerplant ownership, fuel-type, powerplant ability, and generation. Google Earth Engine continuously updates this dataset when the new data became available. This dataset could help solve power sector problems at the global level and help the researcher conduct reliable research. This dataset could help in visualization of the status of the power sector at national, individual, or even at the global powerplant level.

This dataset contains information about worldwide powerplants, so this dataset could help understand the structure and power system of the world at an abstract level and could also help estimate powerplants' impacts on the earth's environment and climate.

3.4.7 GLIMS: Global Land Ice Measurements from Space Dataset

GLIMS stands for Global Land Ice Measurement from Space. This dataset consists of measurements of the world's glaciers captured through satellite and communicated from instruments of the optical satellite. National Snow and Ice Data Center (NSDIC) is an official provider of GLIMS datasets, and the Google Earth Engine data catalogue holds GLIMS datasets of the year 1992 to 2017. GLIMS is an international project of the National Snow and Ice Data Center, and this organization is monitoring and surveying approximately 200,000 glaciers around the world. GLIMS dataset is considered ice-land inventory and provides the velocity of the glacier surface, glacier area measurements, geometry, and elevation of the snow line. GLIMS project usually collects previously mentioned data about glaciers through the aerial photograph, through maps, Reflection Radiometer, Landsat Enhanced Thematic Mapper Plus, and through Advanced Spaceborne Thermal Emission. GLIMS dataset can be used in the identification of change in world climate. Further, this dataset could also help in risk assessment of various natural disasters such as ice avalanches, landslides, and floods. Furthermore, this dataset could also help in the identification of expected temperature changes shortly.

3.4.8 TIGER: US Census 5-digit ZIP Code Tabulation Areas 2010

ZCTA stands for zip codes tabulation areas, and United States Census Bureau developed ZTCA based on census statistics 2000, and the ZCTA dataset was again updated after statistics and reports of census 2010 to meet change need. ZCTA approximates the several census blocks extent, which shares mostly the same zip codes in their addresses. Zipcodes in the US changes after some time and zip codes even spread or cross census block boundaries, state, place, and county; these changes cause a problem for the US postal service. Zipcode tabulation areas (ZCTA) define the boundaries of census blocks based on the similarity of zip codes where US postal service official five digits zip codes are the same in most of the addresses each census block has 30 people. ZCTA also a source of aligning US zip codes with census bureau geography.

ZCTA often the same as zip code, but in some cases, the US postal service changes the zip codes, and the modification of zip codes causes dissimilarity between ZCTP and zip codes census block. Those census blocks which do not possess any addresses, but they are enslaved in one of the zip codes areas, are assigned to any surrounded ZCTA. Those census blocks surrounded by multiple ZCTAs will join one of the ZCTAs based on the most extended common share boundary. ZCTA provides boundaries of multiple census blocks through an approximation of zip codes, this approximation of zip codes could help research organizations in conducting research and can draw reliable results on any disease, quality of air, and on water quality within a well-defined area boundary. ZCTA dataset can be used in business intelligence; businesses can be used this data to customize their policies, strategies, and product offers for specific areas to achieve maximum business objectives. ZCTA dataset can also be used in the making of housing reports and community profiles.

3.4.9 USA EPA Ecoregions Dataset

The United States Environmental Protection Agency is the official supplier of the USA EPA Ecoregions datasets, which are available in the Google Earth Engine data catalogue. USA EPA Ecoregions dataset provides a hierarchical ecoregion classification scheme. This dataset consists of a combination of classification of ecoregions provided by the CEC and the United States Environmental Protection Agency (USEPA). This dataset includes ecoregions classification schemes.

Throughout the USA EPA, the ecoregion dataset is categorized in a series, level I offers a broad ecoregion classification, and level IV provides a comprehensive ecoregion classification. Since the ladder, category III usually holds details on category I and IV. The classification scheme for the Commission for Environmental Cooperation (CEC) normally divides all the North American ecoregions into different levels I, II, and III. Through Tier III and IV, the United States Environmental Protection Agency (USEPA) often separates US-only ecoregions into different forms. Ecoregions typically have populations that are quite close and have identical natural tools. Ecoregions for USA EPA Ecoregion data collection are characterized by abiotic and biotic trend analysis, including hydrological, vegetational, surface, geological, and environmental analysis. It can be used to develop a spatial framework for ecosystems and their components to be monitored, evaluated, researched, and managed.

3.4.10 US Census Tracts + Demographic Profile 2010 Dataset

United States Census Bureau releases geodatabase every ten years, and this database is usually referred to as TIGER. US Census Tracts + Demographic profile dataset usually contains demographic data aggregates by census tracts. Census tracts, usually referred to as census areas and census tracts can vary in size at different geographic locations. It might be the extent to city, town, or state. Census tracts are more extensive than in the size of census blocks. A single census tract might consist of people between 2500 to 8000.

This dataset available in Google Earth Engine in tabular form; this dataset provides demographic information of various census tracts. This dataset can be used in the allocation of legislative seats based on demographic data. Further, this dataset can help in deciding the number of officials for various governmental units based on the population size of the geographical area. This dataset can also help in the allocation of resources, and the census of housing can also provide changes in the quality of housing and other facilities, which could help planners in developing the future for housing needs.

3.4.11 TIGER: US 2018 Census States Dataset

United States Census Bureau is the official provider of this dataset, this dataset available in Google Earth Engine as in the form of a vector dataset. This dataset contains 2018 US state's boundaries data and some other information about the United

States' divisions at the governmental level. Each feature of this dataset represents state or state equivalent. Additionally, this dataset also includes statistical data of the U.S. Virgin Islands, American Samoan Islands, Columbia, and Puerto Rico districts. This dataset can be used in the estimation of the population growth of different US states shortly. This estimation could help planners in resource distribution planning of governmental. Further, this dataset can also help planners identify states that people prefer to move in, so identifying this trend will help planners plan more resources and develop different strategies for non-preferable states. Further, this dataset could also help in finding death ratios of different US states; based on the death ratio, government planners can plan more advanced health facilities in those states where death ratio is high.

3.4.12 TIGER: US 2018 Census Counties Dataset

US 2018 Census Counties dataset consists of boundaries information of US state divisions. These state divisions are usually referred to as counties. Usually, counties perform a governmental role in their areas. In various parts of the USA, counties or divisions are being called with different names, such as divisions or counties being called "parishes" in Louisiana. In Alaska, counties are being called as "boroughs," in some parts of the USA, governmental responsibilities are performed directly by city or state. There is no county in the Columbia districts of the USA, but each area is considered equivalent to a county. Virginia, Maryland, Nevada, Missouri are four self-governed states of the USA.

This dataset provides more deep-down boundaries data and other statistical data of states in the form of counties. This dataset can be used in planning demand and supply of water resources based on counties' statistical and boundaries. Livestock, irrigation, and industrial mining planning can be done efficiently and effectively by utilizing this dataset.

3.4.13 TIGER: US 2018 Census Roads Dataset

This U.S. Census Bureau TIGER dataset incorporates all path segments from the 2016 publication, including over 19 million individual line features spanning the U.S., Columbia Region, Puerto Rico, and Island Regions. Attribute reflects the road segment (a continuous linear navigable route connecting to at least one intersection).

Transportation safety evaluation methods can be developed based on Census data. The question that safety evaluation metrics are trying to answer is the expected frequency of crashes under the areawide set of characteristics that can be described using Census data. Safety performance functions (SPFs) are developed to predict vehicle-only (vehicular), pedestrian-vehicle (pedestrian), and bicyclist–vehicle (bicyclist) crashes on the Census tract level. SPFs are statistical models developed to estimate the average crash frequency for the selected entity (intersection, segment, area) as a function of exposure measures (traffic volume and road segment length) and, if the data availability allows, other conditions that characterize transportation network design and operations, and its environment. The general formulation of SPFs follows a negative binomial regression model form as the most common approach to representing count data with overdispersion (Lawson, 2018). The general form of each SPF is as following Eq.1.

$$\theta_j = e^{(\beta_0 + \beta_1 \ln(Exp1_i) + \beta_2 \ln(Exp2_i) + \sum_j \beta_j x_{ij} + \varepsilon_i)} \dots \dots \dots \dots \dots \dots \dots \dots \dots \dots \dots (1)$$

3.4.14 TIGER: US 2018 Census Blocks Dataset

The United States Census Bureau periodically publishes a geodatabase called TIGER. This dataset includes sections of the 2010 census, roughly equivalent to a section of a community. There are just over 11 million polygon elements that span the U.S., Columbia Territory, Puerto Rico, and Island Countries. Statistical regions characterized by noticeable structures such as highways, streams, railroad tracks, and invisible borders such as property lines, community, borough, school district, county boundaries, and narrow line-of-sight stretches of roads. Typically, tiny in location. A row of censuses appears like a city block surrounded by streets on all sides in a community. Census blocks may be extensive, uneven, and surrounded by a range of features in suburban and rural areas, such as highways, streams, and transmission lines. Census blocks in remote areas will cover hundreds of square miles. We uniquely counted with a four-digit block number of census varying from 0000 to 9999 nesting within each census tract nesting within the state and county. The block category is defined by the first digit of the census block total. Block numbers starting with a zero (in category 0 of blocks) relate to water-only zones.

For many business applications, local-scale data is significant. Any businesses use data from the small area as a proxy for household-level data. More important, though, is the opportunity to collect results from the small-area census of non-standard geographic areas, e.g., for areas of business activity. If these data are available, companies may build aggregations of data in fields. The lower the geography level the data are available for, the more innovative companies can build aggregations, and the more precisely they can describe the geographic area.

3.5 Google Earth Engine Vector Datasets Literature Study

In this section, we have discussed the brief literature study on Google Earth Engine vector datasets. The social implications of each vector datasets are discussed in below Table 2. For the literature study, articles were collected against each dataset name from Google Scholar. Preference was given to those articles that utilized the Google Earth

Engine platform, data mining algorithms, GIS techniques, and Artificial Neural Networks for geospatial data analysis.

Table 2 Google Earth Engine Vector Datasets Literature Study

Dataset Name	Dataset Description	Authors	Social Implication/ Article Summary
World Protected Areas	The data collection for World Conservation Areas provides complete and up-to-date details on protected areas around the planet.	(Deguignet et al., 2017)	This research analyzes how many terms converge at the global, regional, and state levels to explain the significance of this phenomenon at various rates. Our studies indicate that about a fifth of the world's protected areas network is listed in more than one way. There were also eight overlapping designations listed by the writers.
International Boundary Polygons	International Boundary Polygons dataset derived from two different datasets one is the Large-Scale International Boundary (LSIB) file, and the other is World Vector Shorelines (WVS) file. This dataset represents the interior and exterior boundaries of a country.	(Goldblatt et al., 2016)	Urbanization frequently takes place in an unpredictable and contradictory way, resulting in a profound shift in ground cover dynamics and land use patterns. Understanding these trends is crucial to establishing urbanizing developed countries' environmentally sound economic growth strategies. In India, the writers introduce a new dataset of 21.030 polygons, manually labelled "built-up" or "non-built" by the authors for supervised image classification and urban area identification.
USGS Watershed Boundary Dataset	USGS Watershed Dataset provides an identification method and subdivides area of drainage. Watershed boundary dataset provides the extent of all possible watersheds located on the earth's surface, which leads the surface water towards the major outlet point (e.g., stream, river).	(Omernik et al., 2017)	Hydrological units provide a handy, yet troublesome regional collection of spatial polygons based on subjectively defined subdivisions at several hierarchical layers of the land surface regions. The dilemma is that it is challenging to chart equal-sized watersheds, basins, or catchments to cover the entire world. They speak as geographic structures about some of the strengths and limitations of watersheds and hydrological systems.
Landsat WRS2 Grid Dataset	WRS is a regional database network, the WRS dataset used as the main satellite data notion network. Landsat sensors track the planet constantly and have reported emissions of energy from the earth's surface worldwide since 1972.	(Lyons and Sheng, 2018)	This paper provides an innovative method to gather pictures for the global mapping of lakes to reduce the seasonality effect while preserving long-term lake surface variation patterns. The authors define the period best after the wet season during the rainy season, utilizing historical meteorological evidence and a simple model of water equilibrium, for each Landsat tile and select photos acquired during this ideal span for mapping the lake's surface.
RESOLVE Ecoregions Dataset	RESOLVE Ecoregions dataset was introduced in the year 2017, RESOLVE Ecoregions map or	(Liu et al., 2018)	The authors developed the Simplified Urban Areas Composite Index (NUACI) protocol and used the Google Earth engine to enable a large variety of Landsat images

	dataset is based on 846 terrestrial ecoregions of our living planet.		to be categorized worldwide. The overall range of our global mapping performance, product accuracy, and consumer specificity are 0.81–0.84, 0.50–0.60, and 0.49–0.61.
WRI Global Plant Database	WRI Global Plant Database contains power plant data collected from worldwide. This dataset is publicly available in the Google Earth Engine data catalogue.	(Hörsch et al., 2018)	This article deals with the description of the network topology, the selection of a European power stations database, and the regionalization of the top-down time-series. It discusses the derivation of sustainable solar and wind output time series from environmental reanalysis datasets as well as the estimation of land-use constraint capacity for renewable energy.
GLIMS: Global Land Ice Measurements from Space Dataset	GLIMS stands for Global Land Ice Measurement from Space. This dataset consists of measurements of the world's glaciers, which are captured through satellite and communicated from instruments of the optical satellite.	(Poliyapram et al., 2019)	Water/ice/land distinction is an important remote sensing activity that analyzes the presence of water, ice on the earth's surface. For this work, the scientists thus adopted a fairly simple method to collect ground-based data for randomly chosen areas all around the planet. The authors then used a simplified variant of the common deep-floating UNet neural network (CNN) method with extended CNN rates, missed connections, and no max layers of pooling. The conceptual model displays improved results on medium-resolution satellite images in contrast with state-of-the-art versions such as UNet and DeepWaterMap used for the same project (Landsat-8).
TIGER: US Census 5-digit ZIP Code Tabulation Areas 2010	ZCTA stands for zip codes tabulation areas, ZCTA defines the extent of census blocks through an approximation of zip codes.	(Pinheiro et al., 2019)	A Health Service Area (HSA) is a cluster with places served by related healthcare services. The concept of HSAs plays a critical role in characterizing health services accessible in a community, allowing greater planning and management of the health services. The authors in this study contrasted HSA delineations created by the use of broad datasets for population detection algorithms, including various categories of hospital-patient discharges in the US, spanning seven years.
USA EPA Ecoregions Dataset	USA EPA Ecoregions dataset provides a hierarchal classifications scheme of ecoregions. This dataset involves a combination of the ecoregion's classifications scheme provided by both CEC and USEPA.	(Christensen et al., 2016)	Small water bodies (SWBs), such as lakes and reservoirs, may have important combined implications on hydrological, biogeochemical and biological systems, owing to their high numbers and biogeochemical activities. However, the spatial distributions of different forms of SWBs, particularly in growing environments, are always unknown. This study illustrates the role of hydrological changes in the concentration of SWB, namely the potential legacy of state wetland

54

			restoration and pond formation activities. In recognizing these modified distributions and trends, the first step to recognize the joint effects of SWB on the various ecological systems in transformed ecosystems.
US Census Tracts + Demographic Profile 2010 Dataset	US Census Tracts + Demographic profile dataset usually contains demographic data aggregates by census tracts. Census tracts usually referred to as census areas.	(Zoraghein et al., 2016)	Temporary processing of population details in specific areas is typically focused on visual interpolation techniques for constructing temporary secure, and effective structures. Cadastral data is used in this analysis to classify residential property and to perimetrically refine the census tracts to get a more accurate estimate of a small area.
TIGER: US 2018 Census States Dataset	This dataset contains US state boundaries data and some other information about divisions of the United States at the governmental level.	Nil	Nil
TIGER: US 2018 Census Counties Dataset	US 2018 Census Counties dataset consists of boundaries information of US state divisions. These state divisions usually referred to as counties. Usually, counties perform a regulatory role in their areas.	(Edwards et al., 2018)	The analysts utilized recent research on officer fatalities, using Bayesian approaches to measure mortality risk among African, Hispanic, using White people by population and urban region across all U.S. counties.
TIGER: US 2018 Census Roads Dataset	The U.S. Census Bureau TIGER dataset incorporates all route lines from the 2016 publication, including over 19 million individual line features representing the U.S., Columbia County, Puerto Rico, and Island Islands.	(Almotairi et al., 2018)	Many of the newest road maps are vector-like and have specific path points that shape the road segments linking the roads. Nonetheless, for a variety of purposes, program variations between graphs exist. This paper provides a modern distance-inspired method by Hausdorff to prove that the same roads of the applicant in different maps are similar to each other.
TIGER: US 2018 Census Blocks Dataset	This dataset contains the blocks of the 2010 census, roughly equivalent to a section of the community. There are just over 11 million polygon elements spanning parts of the United States, Columbia Territory, Puerto Rico, and the Caribbean.	(Kim, 2018)	The current study suggests novel strategies for allocating established census data on street segments in cities and explores the impact of street segment structural features on crime. This research also measures whether the results of street segment structural properties are comparable with or different from those of walls.

3.6   Image Collection Datasets

The imagery collection of Google Earth Engine provides several ways to view photographs and construct data visualizations, whether they are involved in natural disasters, ground surfaces, water resources, or our oceans. Google Earth Observatory offers earth observation image data at the various high spatial resolution. The public data collection of Earth Engine contains more than forty years of historical images and science databases, modified and extended regularly. The Google Earth Engine data catalogue holds two kinds of datasets: vector datasets and the other is image collection datasets. Image collection datasets are a collection of remote sensing earth observation imagery that is collected or captured at a different period and years. Earth Engine's public data archive contains a different kind of Image collection datasets such as "geophysical data," "Climate and weather data," and "Landsat imagery data." Details of Image collection datasets are given below.

3.6.1 Geophysical Datasets

Geophysical data result from measurements of physical properties. Figure 6 presents different geophysical datasets that are available in the public data catalog of Google Earth Engine, a description of each dataset.

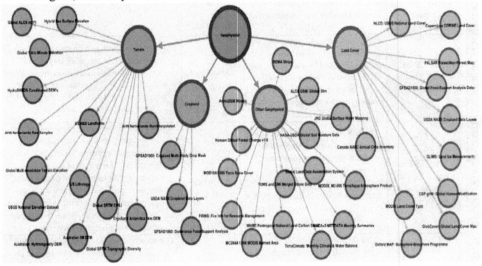

Figure 6 Google Earth Engine Geophysical Datasets Presentation

A literature study on Google Earth Engine geophysical datasets is presented in Table 3. Through a literature study, the social implications of geophysical datasets and technological advancement in the field of geospatial data analysis are discussed below. For the literature study, research articles were collected and selected in the context of Google Earth Engine and geospatial data analysis.

56

Table 3 Google Earth Engine Geophysical datasets literature study

Dataset Name	Dataset Description	Authors	Social Implication/ Article Summary
Hybrid Sea Surface Elevation	HYCOM is a structured ocean model for data assimilative (generalized) hybrid isopycnal-sigma stresses.	(Yusri et al., 2019)	The research goal was to create a script using GEE to generate biologically significant environmental variables from different Earth observation data and models in Indonesia. The geographical and temporal (2002-2017) filters for HYCOM and MODIS AQUA datasets were analyzed and reduced to the maximum, minimum, and mean biologically relevant variables.
AHN Netherlands Non/Interpolated	This model was constructed after the collection of soil samples, and other objects such as trees and bridges and all collected objects are above ground. The regions where missing objects are left vacant and not filled with the interpolated values are un-interpolated. With square reciprocal weighting of lengths, the point cloud was converted into a grid of 0,5 m.	(Hagenaars et al., 2017)	In this analysis, a satellite-derived detection algorithm was built and automatically checked to evaluate the waterline (SDW). The SDWs was linked to standard coastal scales at two sites along the Dutch Sea, where sufficient data of good quality was accessible on-site.
US NED Landforms	US NED landform groups generated using the continuous heat insulation load index (CHILI) coupled with a topographical location index (mTPI) dataset of different scales.	(Oksanen, 2006)	LiDAR data and items may be used during the provisional, data-gathering stage of wetland delineations to display vegetative, topographic, and hydrological trends across a project region and concentrate the inquiry on transitional areas. The authors cannot show hydrophytic plants or hydric soils. While data on LiDAR intensity may provide details on the magnitude of flooding, they do not contain information on the incidence or length of flooding and should not be used as a primary indicator of hydrology. Intensity data collected during the growing season could be used as a secondary hydrology predictor for the wetlands. LiDAR data or goods are not a suitable replacement for a field inquiry.
CryoSat-2 Antarctica 1km DEM	An elevation model of Antarctica ice shelves and ice sheets derived from CryoSat-2 measurements.	(Müller et al., 2016)	Here the writers clarify our attempts to analyze the earth structure possible both now and in deep geological times. The GPlates client (Portal.gplates.org) is a guide to an

			immersive globe set focused on the Cesium JavaScript framework. The database offers a simple, interactive simulation of global geophysical and geological datasets covered by images of the simulated landscape.
Global SRTM Topographic Diversity	This dataset represents the humidity and temperature differences accessible to animals as local habitats. It notes that a greater variety of topo-climatic niches, given climate change, will encourage greater diversity (especially plants) and facilitate the survival of organisms.	(Chen et al., 2017)	This research developed a new classification algorithm. In more depth, these forests were mapped with: (1) greening, vegetation, and tidal floods covering results from Landsat time series and (2) height, slope, and cross-sectional maritime parameters.
Global SRTM CHILI	CHILI is an indicator of insolation and topographical shade in evapotranspiration that is seen by the calculation of sunlight in the early afternoon relative to the sun level. The emphasis is on the 30 meters of SRTM DEM. While these measurements are used in several respects, their main aim was to establish an ecological and chart of landforms and physiographic classes suitable for preparing for climate change.	Nil	Nil
US Lithology	The dataset Lithology contains on-surface classes in the general soil parent element types. It's not an example of DEM.	(Henshaw et al., 2019)	This essay explores how the Google Earth Network aims to research physical structures and processes of the river by the construction of an empirically grounded, far-reaching description of the semi-natural single European flow into intermediate rivers. The authors defined 194 reaches 68 rivers for examination using strict criteria for the selection of images.
Australian 5M DEM	This graph includes a sequence of Geoscience Australia elevation datasets, available under the International Creative Commons License 4.0. The DEM-S represents the topography of the ground surface, minus trees, and was smoothed to minimize noise and enhance surface appearance.	(Donchyts et al., 2016)	Through utilizing the drainage network and Landsat 8 Imagery, authors derived a high-resolution water cap. Our method of deriving a Landsat 8 surface water mask requires the usage of a Landsat 8 (TOA) imagery.
USGS National Elevation Dataset	This dataset presents National Elevation raster data and taken from Alaska, Hawaii, different Sovereign Islands, and the United States. The National Elevation Dataset is taken from different	(Nascetti et al., 2017)	To utilize the high cloud computing and analysis facility of the Google Earth Engine platform, in this research study SRTM and ASTER, the two most commonly used

			DSMs were evaluated in Utah, Nevada, Colorado, Michigan.
Global Multi-resolution Terrain Elevation Data 2010	The edition of the dataset here accessible is Break line Emphasis, arc-second resolution 7.5. Break line emphasis retains fundamental topographical qualities (strips or ridge) within a landscape by keeping on a broken line within the given study period, either the minimum or the maximum elevation value.	(Weiss et al., 2018)	Here, the writers draw up and test a map that quantifies the 2015 period of the cities by integrating ten global surfaces with human activity strength variables and 13,840 urban high-density centres in an established geospatial modelling framework in a spatial resolution of about one kilometre per kilometre.
AHN Netherlands Raw Samples	Every edition contains ground-level products as well as bridges, ground, and trees. The cloud point has been converted into a 0,5 m grid by measuring the opposite distance squared.	(Boer et al., 2012)	This paper has demonstrated that Open Earth has achieved significant importance by covering a wide range of marine and coastal NCK data forms in Google Earth concurrently. Google Earth is an effective tool for grappling with the traditional gulf between professional information and end-users. There are endless resources for NCK recruiting.
HydroSHEDS Conditioned DEM's	This dataset used to map hydrographic details in a standardized format. This dataset provides raster and vector data of river channels, irrigation paths, and coastal boundaries.	(Li et al., 2019)	Through this review, the writers present a different method in the Taihu Basin case study to address the problem of the watershed delineations. Details of rivers, lakes were obtained from Sentinel-2 Imagery on Google Earth Engine (GEE) utilizing the Canny method, instead of DEM.
Global 1 Arc-Minute Elevation	1-minute arc worldwide study of earth surface relief incorporating ground topography and ocean bathymetry. It has been developed from different datasets throughout the world and the region. It consists of two moving bands: ice sheet and foundation rock.	Nil	Nil
Global ALOS mTPI	These datasets distinguish valleys from hills through the elevation data, and it utilized the mean elevation procedure of this purpose.	(Kelley et al., 2018)	In this research study, shade coffee is mapped in forested land of three districts of northern Nicaragua. Google Earth Engine platform was used to identify shade coffee, and Landsat-8 Imagery was used in this research study.
Australian Hydrologically DEM	The model was hydrologically optimized, and drainage was implemented. The DEM-H tracks flux routes and streamlines based on SRTM rates and allows the	(Hakdaoui et al., 2020)	This research shows the possible usage of GEE to store vast volumes of Satellite Imagery, and detailed permanent spatially-temporary saltwater cavities and humidity

	delineation of the catchment and the related hydrological characteristics. Conformity to drainage has provided a consistent description of the hydrological relations of some types of corresponding drainage compliance items. This software provides a DEM ideal for hydrological research like a catchment description and river route.		monitoring by Imlili Sebkha. Optical and radar images were used to identify the positions of Imlilili Sebkha after discovering the hydrological networks underwater.
Cropland multi-study crop mask	The GFSAD provides knowledge of global cropland at high resolution with water usage in the 21st century contributes to global food protection.	(Dong et al., 2016)	By utilized the potential of Landsat-8 imagery and high cloud computing abilities of Google Earth Engine, this research studies provide a high-resolution mapping of paddy rice in Northeastern Asia.
USDA NASS Cropland Data Layers	USDA-NASS provides an ongoing layer of information for the raster, geo-referred, plant-specific soil cover. The CDL system was initiated in 1997 by one nation. Cropland Data Layer Project provides enhanced projections for key national crops, include crop-specific data layer with geo-location development materials.	(Gao and Anderson, 2019)	Through utilizing the potential of Landsat-8, Sentinel-2, and MODIS satellite imagery on the Google Earth Engine platform, this research study provides variability of yield at large scale more efficiently.
Dominance Food Support Analysis	DFSA provides knowledge of global cropland at high resolution with water usage. The map is developed by overlaying these crops with a map of the global irrigated and rainfed cropland provided by remote sensing of the International Water Management Institute.	(Xiong et al., 2017b)	Automated agriculture mapping in Africa through satellite imagery is complex due to limited access and diverse landscape, this issue resolved by authors by applying automated cropland mapping algorithm and reference data was collected through very high-resolution imagery, field visit, and country reports.
ArcticDEM Mosaic	This dataset contains the Arctic digital surface model produced by high computing software at high quality and high resolution.	(Lütjens et al., 2019)	This book explored the benefits, drawbacks, and possible applications of VR for practical and intuitive 3D field simulation. Also, this research developed a workflow to display large-scale VR field datasets for current mid-end units, despite growing volumes of data.
Hansen Global Forest Change v1.6	In this dataset, Landsat image time series details were used to describe the scale and change of the world's forests.	(Gasparini et al., 2019)	For this report, writers use the Tree Canopy Cover 2000 GFC method to determine the best criteria for the 2000 tree mask cover throughout the Amazon basin following the official Brazilian dataset. The authors compared results from the INPE for the same year with a forest cover analysis on maps given

			by the Brazilian Amazon Deforestation Monitoring Project (PRODES) that employed multiple thresholds (10%, 30%, 80%, 90%, 90%, and 95%).
MOD10A1.006 Terra Snow Cover	MODIS Terra Snow Cover dataset contains information about snow albedo, snow cover fraction, and consistency evaluation (QA) at 500m. Data is generated through the snow mapping algorithm.	(Li et al., 2018)	Using the Landsat TM findings as facts, GEE's MODIS snow cover papers were analyzed and examined during the snow seasons. The developers using the GEE JavaScript program to achieve a commodity loss rate filled by MODIS air, the missing number in the snow season, and eventually 88.94% of the average precision of the test sites.
FIRMS: Fire Information for Resource Management System	Fire Information Management System Dataset provides a rostered LANCE fire detection component. LANCE processes the Near Echtzeit (NRT) active fire stations with Thermal Anomalies product. The position of active fire represents the middle of 1-km of a pixel marked with one or more-pixel fires by the algorithm.	(Davies et al., 2008)	This paper explains how the delivery of fire knowledge from satellites over the last six years has grown. FIRMS also extended the number of applications that may access and utilize satellite-based fire knowledge to identify customer needs and to take advantage of recent advances in fields such as database processing, discovery, connectivity, visualization, and supporting technology.
MCD64A1.006 MODIS Burned Area	MODIS Burned Area data package is a regional 500 m gridded system including burned area per-pixel and high-quality results. In each MODIS sheet, the algorithm determines the date of burn for the 500 m grid cells.	(Long et al., 2019)	The authors concentrate on this report, however, on a globally automated approach to mapping burned areas based on Landsat photos. Through utilizing the vast satellite imagery database, as well as Google Earth Engine's high-performance computing capacities.
WHRC Pantropical National Level Carbon Stock Dataset	Pantropical National Level Carbon Stock provides a map that presents the aboveground carbon amount and its spatial distribution for tropical countries.	(Goetz et al., 2009)	The authors give a description and evaluate the relative importance and drawbacks of remote sensing interventions that apply to AGB mapping.
TOMS and OMI Merged Ozone Data	This data collection includes information about how global and national ozone patterns have been observed over the last 25 years.	(Ziemke et al., 2005)	This cycle creates a rare record of 25 years of Pacific ozone mean in three layers of the atmosphere spanning both latitudes and seasons. The data study reveals that the seasonal variations, reliance on latitude, and patterns in these layers are substantially different. The 25-year trend has demonstrated much ozone loss in the lower stratosphere at an altitude of 25 km. Ozone concentrations are 3–4 times more severe in the lower stratosphere in

			mid to high latitudes, relative to the upper stratosphere, while the volume of ozone in the two areas is nearly the same. For the troposphere, TCO indicates a statistically significant upward increase in the poles, but not in the tropics.
TerraClimate: Monthly Climate and Climatic Water Balance	TerraClimate is a monthly data collection on the regional terrestrial surface's climate and atmosphere water balance. This uses climate-friendly interpolation, which incorporates WorldClim high-spatial climatic normals with coarse spatial precision, yet time-changing evidence from the CRUTs4.0 and the 55-year Japanese re-analysis (JRA55).	(Abatzoglou et al., 2018)	The authors validated the TerraClimate spatiotemporal aspects using annual temperature, precipitation, and calculated station data evapotranspiration and an annual runoff of streamflow gages. TerraClimate datasets display an average mean gain in absolute error and improved spatial accuracy compared to gridded datasets with a low resolution.
MACAv2-METADATA Monthly Summaries	Through utilizing the meteorological training dataset, MACA utilized a downscaled method to remove biases in historical data and produce climate model parallel spatial patterns output.	(Mani and Tsai, 2016)	The report addresses potential drainage and confusion resulting from multiple choices of Global Circulation Model (GCM), specific possible pollution scenarios, and separate downscaling methodological approaches for two watersheds in the southern Arkansas and northern Louisiana.
MOD08_M3.006 Terra/Aqua Atmosphere Product	This dataset is an atmosphere global inventory comprising average grid values of atmospheric parameters of 1 x 1 degree daily. Such criteria refer to the particulate properties of ambient aerosol, gross ozone load, surface water vapour, visual and physical cloud properties, and air stability indices.	(Xiong et al., 2017a)	In this research study, authors produced a 30-m cropland extent mapping product on the Google Earth Engine platform through utilizing 10 days of Sentinel-2 and 16 days Landsat satellite imagery.
Global Land Data Assimilation System	This network contains satellite observed and ground-based data materials. It produces ideal fields of land and fluxes utilizing sophisticated ground surface simulation and data assimilation techniques. It encompasses the years 1948-2010 and will be expanded to later years when applicable details become available.	(Zaitchik et al., 2010)	The study presents a fast, computer-efficient source-to-sink (STS) routing system which generates river discharge assessments at measurement locations based on grids runoff production. The authors applied the scheme to the stored performance of the GLDAS as post-processor.
NASA-USDA SMAP Global Soil Moisture Data	This dataset provides soil moisture information across the world at a spatial resolution of 0.25*0.25. This dataset contains surface soil moisture, subsurface soil moisture,	(Jamei et al., 2019)	New data processing approaches are introduced for the Google Earth Engine (GEE) and GIS applications in this article. The GEE model was used for 18 years to measure various variables, including LST,

	and surface soil moisture anomalies.		NDVI, NDBI, temperature, wind speed, evapotranspiration, and soil surface humidity.
JRC Global Surface Water Mapping Layers, v1.1	This dataset contains the distribution and location of surface water temporally, and it also contains statistics of water extent and its surface changes from 1984 to 2018.	(Busker et al., 2019)	The research studied a time series of changes in lake level and river capacity for 137 lakes across all continents between 1984 and 2015, by integrating the DAHITI satellite altimetry database with the JRC Global Surface Water (GSW) dataset. The GSW data collection is a very precise, 30 m resolution surface water dataset, sacrificing the whole L1 T Landsat 5, 7, and 8 files, which makes for very lengthy Google Earth Engine estimation for comprehensive lake area measurements globally.
ALOS DSM: Global 30m	This dataset contains an interactive digital surface model with approximately 30 m (1 arc sect mesh) horizontal resolution. The dataset is based on the World 3D Topographic Data Dataset (5-meter mesh version).	(Santillan et al., 2016)	As an alternative to SRTM-30 m and ASTER GDEM, this work aims at contributing to many studies testing AW3D and developing AW3D30 for highly detailed, flood models and risk-mapping applications.
REMA Strips	This dataset contains Antarctica high-resolution digital surface model with time-stamped at spatial-resolution of 8-m.	Nil	Nil
Canada AAFC Annual Crop Inventory	This dataset provides Ocean Salinity and virtually real-time hourly, two-weekly and monthly Surface Soil Moisture charts, and extracted from the average passive microwave results.	(Yadav and Congalton, 2018)	Global agriculture tracking systems depend on worldwide reliable and timely cropland knowledge. The NASA Creating Earth System Data Records to be Used in Science Environments (MEaSUREs) Software has recently developed three separate spatial resolutions, GFSAD1 km, GFSAD250 m, and GFSAD30 m, global food protection analysis (GFSAD) help data charts. The three GFSAD cropland scale maps have been tested for accuracy and contrasted to evaluate their consistency and reliability on the national and regional scales for cropland monitoring.
MODIS Land Cover Type	This dataset provides yearly interval basis land cover types globally, which are derived through different classification schemes. This product extracted through reflectance data supervised classification.	(Sidhu et al., 2018)	In this paper, the authors investigate the satellite imagery analysis capability of the Google Earth Engine platform by performing analysis on Landsat, GlobCover, and medium resolution Spectroradiometer satellite imagery.

GlobCover: Global Land Cover Map	GlobCover consists of a global land cover map at a resolution of 300m; global land cover is constructed based on MERIS satellite sensor input.	(Giri et al., 2013)	Here, authors produced an advance and next-generation mapping, monitoring, and characterization of land cover at a spatial resolution of 30-m.
CSP gHM: Global Human Modification	This dataset provides a quantitative measure of terrestrial land modification made by humans at a resolution of a 1-Square kilometre.	(Gordon et al., 2005)	In this paper, the authors analyzed water vapour flow changes in the context of future land-use modification, and the results showed major deforestation sub-Saharan regions of Africa and also provides the intensity of agriculture production.
GLIMS: Global Land Ice Measurements	GLIMS is an inventory of global land ice; this dataset consisted of the velocity of snow, elevation line of snow, snow geometry, and other glacier area measurements.	(Raup et al., 2007)	The authors present an example of changes to the GLIMS Glacier database in the Cordillera Blanca glaciers as compared with historical data. The findings indicate substantial improvements in this method over the past 30 years, but also demonstrate the need to develop specific guidelines for remote sensing monitoring of glaciers.
USDA-NASS Cropland Data Layer	This dataset contains crop-specific information about cropland cover data of United States continents, and data is gathered through satellite imagery at moderate resolution.	(Beal Cohen et al., 2019)	This research was conducted to decide whether satellite data would reproduce the effects of rotational activities in field fields. The writers analyzed crop rotation return advantages with satellite imagery forecasts in Indiana, Iowa, and Illinois and contrasted the return benefits with field results from 2007 to 2012.
GFSAD1000: Global Food-Support Analysis Data	DFSA provides knowledge of global cropland at high resolution with water usage.	Nil	Nil
Global PALSAR-2/PALSAR Forest/Non-Forest Map	Through applying classification procedure on SAR image with the backscatter coefficient technique, this dataset provides a map of forest/non-forest classification at a resolution of 25m.	(Qin et al., 2016)	In this research, authors applied rules and pixels-based algorithms to map and identify annual forest in Oklahoma, the USA from 2007 to 2010. FBD, ALOS, and Landsat satellite imagery were used for this purpose.
Copernicus CORINE Land Cover	CORINE Inventory started in 1985 to standardized land data of Europe to the policy development process of the environment. This dataset provides land changes status under the framework of CORINE.	(Bereta et al., 2019)	The writers explore in this paper the problems of massive Copernicus data and how the configured Copernicus seeks to overcome them. The authors also give lessons learned from our Copernicus Device Lab project, which gathers the knowledge on Copernicus resources and renders it accessible

			on the web by leveraging semantic technology for smartphone developers.
NLCD: USGS National Land Cover Database	NLCD is the global ground cover database focused on Landsat, 30-meter resolution. Further, it provides land cover changes database based on multi-temporal. NLCD promotes non-governmental local and projects to assess environmental environments and well-being, identify regional habitat trends, forecast the effects of climate change, and design land management policies.	(Zurqani et al., 2019)	The aims of this analysis were: (1) to establish groups and land cover distribution in stream riparian regions; (2) to evaluate the quality of the current land cover data utilizing high-resolution NAIIP and LiDAR imagery; and (3) to evaluate forested riparian buffer areas in the Drainage of the Lower Savannah River.

3.6.2 Climate and Weather Datasets

Weather simulations produce long-term temperature forecasts as well as historical surface interpolations. The Earth Engine database contains NCEP/NCAR historical reanalysis info, grids such as NLDAS-2 and GridMET info, and climatic model findings such as the University of Idaho MACAv2-METADATA and Downscaled Weather Projection of NASA Earth Exchange. Climate data explains the expected and observed conditions over brief intervals, including weather, temperature, wind, and other variables. Earth Engine covers NOAA Global Forecast System (GFS) and NCEP Climate Forecast System (CFSv2) forecast results, as well as sensor details from sources such as the TRMM (Tropical Rainfall Measuring Mission). Figure 7 shows a Google Earth Engine climate and weather dataset visualization and shows a list of climate datasets and weather datasets in Gephi software. Below is a description of each dataset.

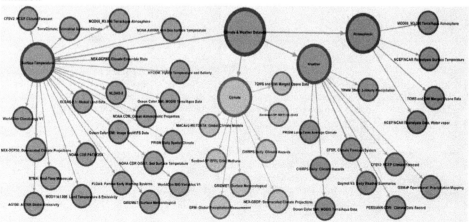

Figure 7 Google Earth Engine Climate & Weather Datasets Presentation

The literature study was conducted on Climate & Weather datasets of the Google Earth Engine. As a result of the literature study, the social implications of Climate & Weather datasets and technological advancements in the field of geospatial data analysis are presented in following Table 4. For the literature study, research articles were collected and selected in the context of Google Earth Engine and geospatial data analysis.

Table 4 Literature Study on Google Earth Engine Climate & Weather Datasets

Dataset Name	Dataset Description	Authors	Social Implication/ Article Summary
CFSV2: NCEP Climate Forecast	It is the same model used to generate the NCEP Climate Prediction Method Reanalysis (CFSR), and the CFSv2 dataset aims to improve the CFSR.	(Feng et al., 2018)	Calibrated and corrected Landsat 8 image composites for the whole island were generated by the use of the Google Earth Engine for a comparable period of phenology before and after Maria.
TerraClimate: Terrestrial Surface Climate	TerraClimate is a data compilation on the global terrestrial surfaces' monthly climate and atmosphere equilibrium. It combines high-spatial climate resolution climatic standards from WorldClim.	(Abatzoglou et al., 2018)	The authors checked TerraClimate's spatiotemporal dimensions through the usage of annual temperature, precipitation, and measured station data comparison and annual stream-flow calculation. TerraClimate datasets demonstrated an average change in the mean absolute error and improved spatial accuracy compared to the gridded datasets with a grosser resolution.
MOD08_M3.006 Terra/Aqua Atmosphere	This dataset is a global atmosphere commodity that contains average grid values of atmospheric parameters of 1 x 1°per month. Such metrics apply to ambient aerosol particle properties, cumulative ozone load, precipitation of the environment, visual and physical cloud properties, and air stability indices.	Nil	Nil
NOAA AVHRR 4KM Sea Surface Temperature	NOAA AVHRR is a collection of 4km global surface temperature of the sea, which is captured twice daily.	(Medina-Lopez and Ureña-Fuentes, 2019)	This research seeks to obtain high-resolution marine surface salinity (SSS) and global ocean temperature (SST) values by the use of direct satellite data (i.e., pre-processing or air correction without band results). Sentinel-2 Level 1-C Reflectance data (TOA) is used for correct SSS and SST data.
NEX-DCP30: Climate Ensemble Stats	This dataset provides corrected, and high-resolution projections of climate change from 1950 to 2005; climate change projections can be used to evaluate the impact of climate change on climate-sensitive processes.	(Davis et al., 2017)	The authors formed the standard fire climate in the Pacific North West area of the US for major forest fires (> 40 ha). Extensive forest fire frequency data from the historical environment model duration (1971-2000) have been used as predictive

			variables for response vector and precipitation for fire season, high temperature, slope, and elevation.
HYCOM: Hybrid Temperature and Salinity	HYCOM is an isopycnal-stomatology (generalized) data-assimilative ocean-coordinate model. The HYCOM data sub-set hosting in EE includes the salinity, temperature, speed, and lifting variables. They were interpolated between 80.48°S and 80.48°N on a standard 0.08-degree lat/long scale.	(Tung and Son)	This research has been conducted to find the best locations for Japanese scallop hanging communities using multi-criteria assessment models focused on geographical information systems (GIS). Parameters were determined through remote sensing data.
Ocean Color SMI: MODIS Terra/ Aqua Data	This dataset consists of ocean and ocean color biology data derived from EOSDIS; this dataset can be used in studying diversity change, coastal zones hydrology, biology, and marine habitats distribution.	(Pottier et al., 2006)	The weighted average and unbiased study have been evaluated and applied to two methods for the ocean colour mixing in the Northern and Equatorial Atlantic Basins. The datasets were then binned regular chlorophyll-a chlorophyll results from the SeaWiFS and Aqua satellite with a low-resolution signal spectroradiometer in the year 2003, the first standard year of operations.
NLDAS-2	LDAS dataset provides Earth surface climatological properties; it is produced by different observations such as satellite data, satellite or radar precipitation.	(Wang et al., 2014)	This article presents a comprehensive data analysis framework for soil moisture assimilations that are driven by C language. The program offers the automated operation, effective visualization of graphs, and the study of land surface details. The program will increase the quality of control of data assimilation and incorporate data collection and interpretation capabilities comprehensively into the GIS production framework.
GLDAS-2.1: Global Land Data	Uses a surface and remotely sensed computer network, land surface models, and data assimilation approaches to provide terrestrial data. The production contains properties of soil moisture and is an outstanding predictor of drought.	(Jurkowski et al., 2019)	Information from sensors on various NASA satellites, including Landsat 8, Aqua, and Terra, is employed by models included in this analysis. In fall 2018, the NASA Establish Idaho Water Management II team validated two versions, the Operational Simplified Surface Energy Balance (SSEBop) and the High-Resolution Imaging Spectroradiometer (MODIS) Regional ET Project (MOD16).
NOAA CDR: Ocean Atmospheric Properties	NOAA CDR dataset provides climate data such as the temperature of the air, speed of the wind, and ocean surface humidity.	(Privette et al.)	This project aims to supplement and sustain regular progress achieved by CDR function in NOAA and other federal agencies, e.g., NASA, USGS, the CDR project is focused

			on helping us explain Earth's water and energy cycles.
Ocean Color SMI: Image SeaWiFS Data	This dataset consists of ocean and ocean color biology data derived from EOSDIS, and this dataset can be used in studying diversity change, coastal zones hydrology, biology, and marine habitats distribution.	(Swartz et al., 2010)	This method enabled us to allocate operating status to an ocean grid network with 0.5° latitude/longitude and to monitor improvements in its status over 56 years. The trend indicates the massive extension of marine harvesting from North and West Pacific coastal areas to the oceans of the southern hemisphere and high seas.
PRISM Daily Spatial Climate	PRISM dataset provides daily or monthly climate data in the form of grids. Grids are built using Independent Slopes System Parameter Elevation Regressions (PRISM). PRISM interpolation procedures model how extreme weather and atmosphere vary, and coastal impacts are taken into consideration.	(Daly et al., 2007)	This article introduces the creation, implementation, and evaluation of methods to create high-resolution regular weather grids. The elevations ranged from 194 to 1650 m within the USSW. The meteorological simulation components were minimum and maximum levels, gross ice, ice and snowfall, and average solar radiation and radiation.
NOAA CDR OISST: Sea Surface Temperature	NOAA offers total ocean temperature areas created by integrating bias-adjusted measurements from multiple sources (satellites, aircraft, boats) on the standard global grid, with interpolated holes. Primary input data of AVHRR satellite which allows for broad time/space coverage from late 1981 to the present day.	(Vose et al., 2012)	This paper explains the latest version of the Merged Land-Ocean Surface Temperature (MLOST Release 3.5) study used for organizational tracking and temperature evaluation. The key explanation for the current update is to provide a modern land dataset with numerous major changes, including a more nuanced method to tackle station adjustment, instrumentation, and position conditions.
NOAA CDR PATMOSX	This dataset provides a record of cloud data with multiple cloud properties and also provides reflectance and temperature brightness with AVHRR.	(Foster et al., 2016)	The authors using three reanalysis items in this regard: CFSR, MERRA, and European Middle Age Weather Forecasting Center (ECMWF). As auxiliary data sources of the PATMOS-x/AVHRR Cloud CDR, ERA-Interim (ERA-I) conducts interconnections to assess how sensitive the atmosphere is to pick an ancillary data source.
WorldClim BIO Variables V1	This dataset is derived from monthly rainfall and temperature to produce more meaningful biological values. Bioclimatic variables consist of annual temperature range and precipitation, warmest, and coolest month.	(Fick and Hijmans, 2017)	In this article, the authors describe the newly created global high spatial resolution dataset of land climate monthly data.

GRIDMET: Surface Meteorological	The Gridded Surface Meteorological Dataset accounts for average surface temperature, precipitation, climate, moisture, and radiation fields with broad spatial precision (~4 km) throughout the USA. The dataset combines PRISM spatial data with National Land Data Assimilation System (NLDAS) to generate continuous fields spatially and temporally that are ideal for additional land surface modeling.	(Huntington et al., 2017)	This article introduced a web application software 'Climate Engine' for high cloud computing processing of Big Data by utilizing the Google Earth Engine interface. Also, this article introduced several research results related to drought and agriculture conducted on Climate Engine.
FLDAS: Famine Early Warning Systems	The FLDAS data kit has been developed to facilitate evaluations of food protection in developing countries having sparse data. This dataset also includes information on average precipitation, soil moisture content, and average soil.	(Liou and Mulualem, 2019)	This report offers useful knowledge to classify areas with the potential of drought and to prepare emergency relief steps. Also, it provides the findings of the first attempt to implement a newly created formula for tracking drought conditions, the Standardized Difference Latent Heat Index (NDLI).
MOD11A1.006 Land Temperature & Emissivity	The result MOD11A1 V6 has regular terrestrial values of surface emissivity and temperature in the form of 1200 by 120 grids. Beyond the latitude of 30 degrees, some pixels can have several observations in which clear sky criteria are met. The pixel count, as this happens, is the sum of all qualified remarks.	(Khan et al., 2020b)	The goal of this analysis was to track the time and space drought variability in the Potohar Plateau (22.254 km2 rainfed area), Punjab, in Pakistan, between 2000 and 2015 by using remote sensing Google Earth Engine database.
AG100: ASTER Global Emissivity	This dataset provides mean emissivity, standard deviation, and means of surface temperature and normalized difference vegetation index with a water mask of land.	(Hulley et al., 2015)	In this article, the authors mapped the emissivity of the earth at a spatial resolution of 100m.
RTMA: Real-Time Mesoscale	The mapping of RTMA for near-surface weather conditions consists of a broad spatial and temporal resolution study. At a range of 2.5km, this dataset also provides hourly CONUS measurements.	(Blankenau, 2017)	This research analyzed the consistency of ETref gridded forecast forecasts. For this evaluation to be carried out, multiple gridded weather datasets – GLDAS-1, NLDAS-2, CFSv2 operational research, GRIDMET, RTMA, and NDFD – were correlated with the data from the weather stations that were deemed "ground-truth" in the United States continental. The stations have been selected as reference conditions, if possible.
NEX-DCP30: Downscaled Climate Projections	This dataset provides projections of the earth's monthly climate from the period of 1950 to 2005.	(Egan and Mullin, 2016)	Here the authors demonstrate that the environmental patterns endured by the vast majority of the people of the United States changed from

			1974 to 2013. Based on prior studies on the effect of environment on local population development, investigators found that 80% of Americans reside in areas that are in improved conditions than four decades ago.
WorldClim Climatology V1	This dataset provides monthly mean: Minimum and maximum temperature and emissivity of the globe.	(Koulgi et al., 2019)	In this article, vegetation condition was analyzed in the Tiger Reserves area of India through the utilization of Landsat-5 data.
MACAV2-METADATA: Global Climate Models	Through utilizing meteorological training, the dataset, MACA, utilized a downscaled method to remove biases in historical data and produce climate model parallel spatial patterns output.	(Potter et al., 2018)	The writers demonstrate the benefits of a successful rim method in the west of the United States, where the grain mix and temperature regimes are somewhat different. While current approaches are preferred to research other areas, the authors show the benefits of matching this kind of region. The authors consider the projected climate in 2040, 2060, and 2080 and conclude that the projected climate in fruitful rims will lead to increased productivity because of hotter temperatures on average.
Sentinel-SP OFFL CH4: Methane	This dataset provides high-resolution offline methane concentration imaging. Methane (CH_4) is the second contributor to the anthropogenically intensified greenhouse effect following carbon dioxide (CO_2). Approximately three-quarters of methane emissions are anthropogenic, and satellite-based monitoring records are thus necessary to start.	(Irzak et al.)	Automatic learning methods were used to assess the extent of this climate risk and to inform the use of mitigation strategies. The authors aim to (1) calculate the number of dispersed methane infiltrations, (2) approximate the intensity of their movement, and (3) explain how they are modified at through tempers by integrating the computer-based vision-assisted study of satellite data with detailed field steps.
GRIDMET: Surface Meteorological	The Gridded Surface Meteorological Dataset accounts for average surface temperature, precipitation, climate, moisture, and radiation fields with broad spatial precision (~4 km) throughout the USA. This dataset combines PRISM data with National Land Data Assimilation System (NLDAS) to generate continuous fields spatially and temporally that are ideal for additional land surface modelling.	(Cho et al., 2019)	In this research article, the Random Forest Machine Learning classifier was used to identify the subsurface drainage system with its expansion.
GPM: Global Precipitation Measurement	This dataset provides worldwide estimates and observations of snow and rain after every three hours, GPM	(Appel and Pebesma, 2019)	This paper proposes on-demand data cubes designed on the fly as computer users process results. The

	satellite utilized Integrated Multi-satellite Retrievals algorithm for providing rainfall estimates.		authors describe the open-source C++ framework and R "gdalcubes" software for the creation and analysis of on-demand data cubes from satellite image collections and how it facilitates dynamic method production workflows where data users may first attempt methods on limited subsamples before running high-resolution or wide areas analyzes. The author
NEX-GDPP: Downscaled Climate Projections	The NASA NEX-GDDP data collection comprises of downscale global environment simulations originating from the GCM runs in two of the 4 greenhouse gas pollution scene simulations, defined as Member Concentration Pathways.	(Erickson et al., 2017)	This research shows that calculating and sharing climate indexes using cloud computing technology from global downscaled climate projection datasets is feasible. Throughout the future, environment indexes will be available to current users via the GEE API.
CHIRPS Daily: Climate Hazards	CHIRPS is a quasi-global precipitation dataset of 30 years and more. CHIRPS utilize 0.05°in-site satellite imagery to establish a gridded precipitation time series for regional drought and pattern research.	(Sazib et al., 2018)	In this research article, authors utilized soil moisture datasets available on the Google Earth Engine to monitor drought and also for crop forecasting.
Sentinel-5P NRTI CLOUD	This dataset includes high-resolution cloud parameter imagery for NRTI.	(Valade et al., 2019)	The authors introduce the Space Instability Tracking Network (MOUNTS) for Volcano Surveillance, targeted at global monitoring. It's carried out through the use of multisensory satellite imagery.
TOMS and OMI Merged Ozone Data	This dataset provides findings for the tracking of global and national ozone levels throughout the past 25 years.	(Chehade et al., 2014)	Statistical trends and systematic analysis of ozone datasets were provided in this study, and datasets were collected from different sources.
TRMM 3B42: 3-Hourly Precipitation	The TRMM is a collaborative NASA-Japan Aerospace Exploration Agency (JAXA) project aimed at tracking and analyzing tropical rainfall. Agriculture is primarily dominated by rainfall in tropical lowlands (Yemen, Saudi Arabia, the UAE, and Southeast Asia). For these regions, certain climate elements and temperatures for particular are relatively stable both on a location and over time, yet the precipitation differs even more.	(Nivedita Priyadarshini et al., 2019)	This study analyzed land cover changes after pre and post-cyclone by utilizing SAR datasets.
CFSR: Climate Forecast System	This dataset provides a high-resolution ocean sea ice atmospheric forecast. It has been extended as a real-time operational product. Four	(Lensky et al., 2018)	Here authors analyzed the role of dynamics of vegetation, seasonality, and circulation of synoptic-scale by using heat estimates and normalized

	times a day (0000, 0600, 1200, and 1800 UTC) are initialized.		difference vegetation index of the satellite.
Daymet V3: Daily Weather Summaries	This dataset offers a forecast for the USA, Mexico, Canada, Hawaii, and Puerto Rico in gridded with regular environment parameters. It emerges from collected data from meteorological stations and different data outlets. Daymet V3 utilizes an entirely different set of inputs relative to the previous edition, including: • Land/Water Mask: MODIS 250 MOD44W_v2. NASA_ORNL_ • The Horizon files derive from SRTM DEM. • NASA SRTM DEM version 2.1.	(Muche et al., 2019)	As weather data outlets, the writers contrasted four gridded databases (DAYMET, NLDAS, GLDAS, and PRISM). In comparison to a calculated dataset, the authors assessed how hydrological model efficiency was influenced by the Global Historical Climatology Network-Daily (GHCN-D) Delaware River study was performed at Perry Dam, eastern Kansas.
PERSIANN-CDR: Climate Data Record	This dataset provides partial global precipitation since 1983; quarterly precipitation is recorded.	(Wang et al., 2019)	By measured the flood frequency with a Google Earth Engine (GEE) index and pixel water detection algorithm, this analysis investigated the spatial-temporal variability of the lake from 1988 to 2016. It contrasted the water body variations between the pre- and post-TGD cycles of Poyang Lake. The lake's year-long water supply has seen a substantial decline over the past 29 years and has switched into a narrower structure since 2006.
GSMap Operational: Precipitation Mapping	The Global Precipitation Satellite Mapping (GSMaP) produces a regional hourly rainfall with a range of 0.1 x 0.1 degrees. Values are measured using GPM Core Observatory satellite multi-band passive microwave and infrared radiometers and with the aid of a network of other satellites. The precipitation intensity recovery algorithm of GPM is based on a model for radiative transfer. The modified rate of precipitation is determined based on the 24-hour total of GSM hourly rainfall by calculating the NOAA/CPC gages.	(Ushio and Kachi, 2010)	In this article, Kalman model-based approach was utilized with Global Precipitation Satellite Mapping to produce an accurate estimated perception of earth.

NCEP/NCAR Reanalysis Surface Temperature/ Water Vapor	This joint initiative is aimed at generating new analyzes of the environment utilizing historical records and examining the existing condition of the environment (Climate Data Assimilation Method, CDAS). The NCEP/NCAR Reanalysis 1 project utilizes an innovative analysis/prediction method to conduct data assimilation from 1948 to the present using historical results.	(Parastatidis et al., 2017) (Xianzhou et al., 2017)	1. In this article, Landsat 5, 7, 8, and other emissivity datasets from different sources were utilized to estimate land surface temperature. 2. In this research, the elevation dependence of climate change was investigated with four separate measurements and reanalysis sets for China. There was a lack of continuity regarding heating and elevation around the Tibetan plateau and China.

3.6.3 Imagery Datasets

High-resolution photography shows images of environments and cityscapes. Satellite imaging (also Earth observation images or spatial photography) is an image of the Earth or other planets collected by government and business satellites around the world. The satellite image resolution varies depending on the instrument and the satellite's orbit altitude. For instance, the Landsat database provides replicated 30-meter resolution photographs to the earth, but most of them have not been processed from raw data. Landsat 7 has an average 16-day return period. Photos with a resolution of 41 cm will be used for much smaller regions. When discussing satellite images in remote sensing, there are four types of resolution: spatial, spectral, temporal, radiometric, and geometric.

The pixel size of an image, reflecting the region of the surface (i.e., m2) measured on the ground by instantaneous field of view (IFOV) sensors, is known as a spatial resolution; the temporal resolution is described by time (i.e., days), which moves through image processing times for a given surface location. Radiometric resolution is a function of an imaging device for capturing multiple degrees of brightness (for example contrast), and the efficient bit-depth (grayscale level number) of the sensor, normally as 8-bit (0–255), 11-bit (0–2047), 12-bit (0–4095), or 16-bit (0–65,535).

Geometric resolution relates to the satellite sensor's capacity to view a portion of the earth's surface accurately in a single-pixel, which usually corresponds to the ground sample distance or GSD. GSD is a concept for both visual and environmental noise sources. It is helpful to measure how effectively a sensor will 'sense' an entity with a single pixel on the field. Following Figure 8, Earth Engine imagery datasets are visualized in Gephi tools.

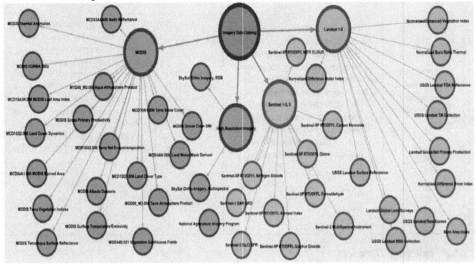

Figure 8 Google Earth Engine Imagery Datasets Presentation in Gephi

A literature study on social implications of Google Earth Engine imagery datasets and technological advancement in the field of geospatial analysis is discussed in the following Table 5. For the literature study, research articles were collected and selected in the context of Google Earth Engine and geospatial data analysis.

Table 5 Literature Study on Google Earth Engine Imagery Datasets

Dataset Name	Dataset Description	Authors	Social Implication/ Article Summary
MCD43A4.006 Nadir Reflectance	This dataset provides a bidirectional reflectance distribution feature. This software incorporates data from both the spacecraft Terra and Aqua, selecting the strongest representative pixel from 16 days. The original data is described in sine projection.	(Xie et al., 2019a)	This article proposes an automated land-cover classification mechanism utilizing Landsat imagery data.
MODIS Thermal Anomalies	The MOD14A1 V6 dataset provides composites with a regular fire mask range of 1 km from 4 and 11-micrometre radiance MODIS.	(Hu and Hu, 2019)	This study, supported by the Google Earth Engine (GEE), used Landsat imagery by satellite and selected random forest algorithms for land

			classification and annual Central Asian land cover data from 2001 to 2017. The distribution and dynamic patterns of land cover were summarized based on the temporal datasets, and the key factors which drive land changes were analyzed.
MODIS FORMA Data	FORMA is a 2-monthly deforestation alert system based on MODIS 500 x 500 meters for humid tropical forests. The Earth Engine FORMA 500 data collection is a picture with warnings beginning in January 2006 and monthly updates. An increasing warning is correlated with a period in units of epochal seconds in a single band called an alarm date. Filtering FORMA by dates and measuring warnings inside areas of concern are two of the most important tasks that the FORMA dataset can do.	(Joshi et al., 2016)	Use a modern satellite tracking network; the writers analyzed for the survival of wild tigers 14 years of forestry data in 76 ecosystems (ranging from 278 to 269.983 km2. Our study updates tiger habitat status and identifies the latest technical technologies to predict reliably where forest destruction happens to minimize potential habitat degradation.
MCD15A3H.006 MODIS Leaf Area Index	This data collection contains the leaf zone index provided by the two-way reflectance factor Terra and Aqua (BRF).	(Gao et al., 2012)	This technique utilizes MODIS to generate a regression tree comparing these MODIS LAI observations to land-sat surface reflections in a homogeneous and high-quality LAI recuperation. The results indicate that the method may deliver reliable estimates of Landsat's LAI, as measured by field measurements collected during the 2002 soil moisture experiment in central Iowa throughout rapid vegetation development.
MYD08_M3.006 Aqua Atmosphere Product	This dataset provides average grid values of atmospheric parameters of 1*1-degree. Such metrics apply to ambient aerosol particle properties, cumulative ozone load, precipitation of the environment, visual and physical cloud properties, and air stability indices. The software also	(Mao et al., 2018)	In this article, the ice cloud's vertical response was investigated during the monsoon season of Indian from 2006 to 2010.

	includes methods, regular variances, weighted QA figures, log-normal distributions, estimates of variability, and figures on fractions of pixels that follow those criteria.		
MODIS Gross Primary Productivity	The data collection draws on the principle of radiation efficiency, which can be used as sources for data models for earth resources, biomass, water cycle processes that plant biogeochemistry.	(He et al., 2018)	In this research study, seven different crop yields estimated annually across Montana, USA.
MOD10A1.006 Terra Snow Cover	This dataset provides snow cover, albedo, and a fractional cover of snow with an assessment of quality.	(Eythorsson et al., 2019)	In this article, the impact of climate change was assessed on Arctic snow resources.
MCD12Q2.006 Land Cover Dynamics	This dataset predicts the timing of global vegetation phenology. It also includes details on the spectrum and summation of the EVI measured from MODIS surface reflectiveness data for each pixel.	(Huang et al., 2017)	Throughout this analysis, the authors used the NDVI pathway to identify significant land distribution patterns throughout Beijing. Throughout 2015, throughout Google Earth Engine (GEE), the developers also listed ground cover forms. The authors calculated the principal types of land cover evolving by overlaying the new forms of land cover and spatial distribution of land cover dynamics. The overall change detection for three types (vegetation loss due to adverse NDVI changes, vegetation gain associated with positive NDVI changes, and no changes) is 86.13%.
MOD16A2.006 Terra Net Evapotranspiration	At a resolution of the 500-meter pixel, this dataset provides latent heat and evapotranspiration with the usage of MODIS 16 data.	(Lauer et al., 2018)	The project used modeled data from the Evapotranspiration Flow (EEFlux) of the Google Earth Engine, and the Simplified Surface Energy Balance (SSEBop), MODIS Global ET Project (MOD16). The NLDAS-2 Noah model has the highest in situ association with the RCEW, with an

			average determination factor of RP 2P = 0.87.
MODIS Ocean Color SMI	This dataset consists of biology data of ocean and ocean colour derived from EOSDIS; this dataset can be used in studying diversity change, coastal zones hydrology, biology, and marine habitats distribution.	(Pottier et al., 2006)	The weighted average and unbiased study have been evaluated and applied to two methods for the ocean colour mixing in the Northern and Equatorial Atlantic Basins. The datasets were then binned regular chlorophyll-a chlorophyll results from the Wide-Field-of-View Sensor (SeaWiFS) and the Aqua satellite with low-resolution signal spectroradiometer in the year 2003, the first standard year of operations.
MOD44W.006 Land Water Mask Derived	The products of the MOD44W V6 land/water mask 250 m are derived using a MODIS-trained, validated MOD44W V5 Decision Tree Classifier. A variety of masks are used to fix identified issues created by landscape colours, burn wounds, cloudiness, or ice protection in oceans.	(Bevington et al.)	This article describes NASA World Wind, a product used to visualize burned area products produced through MODIS.
MCD64A1.006 MODIS Burned Area	This dataset provides monthly 500m quality information and per-pixel based burned area. The VI is extracted from MODIS shortwave infrasound surface reflectance bands 5 and 7 with period texture estimation.	(Boschetti et al., 2008)	This article explains how NASA World Wind, a simulated open-source globe, is currently used to view MODIS's burned region result. The methods for translating the sample into a World Wind compliant format and the spatial generalization of such data are defined at various scales. Instructions for receiving and utilizing simulation photos of the MODIS burned region component in World Wind are provided.
MODIS Albedo Datasets	The Albedo Design Dataset MCD43A3 V6 is a 16-day offering every day. With each surface mirror band (Band 1 through Band 7), the reflectance produces both directional (Black Sky Albedo) and bi-hemispheric (White Sky Albedo) reflectance,	(Mitraka et al., 2016)	This data collection has been used here for the LSA approximation and its 0.5 km spatial resolution adjustments across the sample region. The MODIS albedo tool of both the directional-

	as well as three broad-spectrum bands (visible, near-infrared, short wave). Each picture of 500m/pixel per day is generated using 16 days of data based on the given day.		hemispheric surface reflection (black-sky albedo) as well as the bi-hemispheric (white-sky albedo) surface reflection was employed. The LSA is estimated for the entire world on an 8-day basis for the entire MODIS acquisition period (i.e., 2000 up to now).
MCD12Q1.006 Land Cover Type	This dataset provides yearly interval basis land cover types globally, which are derived through different classification schemes. This product is extracted through reflectance data supervised classification.	(Sidhu et al., 2018)	In this paper, the authors investigate the satellite imagery analysis capability of the Google Earth Engine platform by performing analysis on Landsat, GlobCover, and medium resolution Spectroradiometer satellite imagery.
MODIS Terra Vegetation Indices	This dataset provides the value of vegetation index based on per pixel.	(Long et al., 2019)	However, in this report, the authors rely on an integrated global approach to burned field mapping focused on Landsat pictures. Through leveraging the vast satellite imagery collection and Google Earth Engine's high-performance processing power, the writers suggest an integrated pipeline to produce a world-class 30 m annual burnt area chart of a Landsat picture sequence in a global resolution. The GABAM 2015 launches a revised 30 m annual Global Burned Area Map for 2015.
MOD08_M3.006 Terra Atmosphere Product	This dataset includes an average grid value of 1*1 of the parameters of the atmosphere. Such metrics apply to ambient aerosol particle properties, cumulative ozone load, precipitation of the environment, visual and physical cloud properties, and air stability indices. The software also includes methods, regular variances, weighted QA figures,	(Elhacham and Alpert, 2016)	Although earlier work in the area of Dubai focused primarily on the impacts on the sea or ground, the authors study the atmospheric dynamic effects in a broader field, including land and water. In most recently urbanized areas, increased temperature, as well as decreased albedo, were

78

	log-normal distributions, estimates of variability, and figures on fractions of pixels that follow those criteria.		observed. Temperature fluctuations in both land and sea are often correlated with moisture and wind speed shifts analyzed in many weather stations by the coastal breezes.
MODIS Surface Temperature/Emissivity	The result MOD11A1 V6 has regular terrestrial values of surface emissivity and temperature in the form of 1200 by 120 grids. Beyond the latitude of 30 degrees, some pixels can have several observations in which clear sky criteria are met. The pixel count, as this happens, is the sum of all qualified remarks.	(Bartkowiak et al., 2019)	The nonlinear relation between coarse MODIS LST (CR) resolution and excellent resolution (FR) explaining variables was established by building three distinct models, including (i) all pixels (BM), (ii) only pixels with vegetation content exceeding 90% (EM1) and (iii) with 75% homogeneity of vegetated soil cover class (EM2).
MODIS Terra/Aqua Surface Reflectance	This dataset estimates and adjusted surface spectral reflectance for air substances such as gasses, aerosols, and radiation dispersal.	(Beaton et al., 2019)	The primary purpose of this analysis was to establish a system for producing breakdown dates dataset. A second goal was to derive statistics from this dataset, which can be used to provide interpretations for near-real-time imaging research and to increase comprehension of ice processes in the field of study.
MOD44B.051 Vegetation Continuous Fields	This dataset provides a global surface cover of vegetation at a sub-pixel level.	(Clark and Aide, 2011)	In this research article, the authors discuss and describe the technical capabilities of VIEW-IT web software used to interpret high-resolution satellite imagery visually.
SkySat Ortho Imagery, RGB	This dataset is available in a Multispectral/Pan 5-band array as well as a Pansharpened RGB set. This RGB set contains pictures of three 8-bit pan-sharpened lines. This dataset provides information about response events of the various crisis.	(Murthy et al., 2014)	This paper contains details regarding the SkySat-1 mission, which is the first commercial earth-observation program for microsatellite satellites to produce panchromatic imagery in sub-meter resolution, in addition to 4-band pan-sharpened pictures. SkySat-1 was

			designed and launched on a lower cost order than comparable tasks. The low-cost architecture helps the installation of a large picture telescope with high time resolution and high spatial resolution.
SkySat Ortho Imagery, Multispectral	Interactive orthoimages are helpful for visual perception and traditional applications of visualization. The related panchromatic orthoimages, which are useful for visual perception, machine learning, and algorithm training, are also included. The photos of SkySat have a resolution of 0.8 meters per pixel and a location precision of fewer than 10 meters CE90.	(Mohite et al., 2019)	The authors suggest in this analysis a system for early season cartography of the wheat region utilizing the combined usage of temporal Sentinel-1 and 2 observations. The authors also propose a tool for estimating the parameter of crop phenology viz. Sowing date using a Standardized Variance Vegetation Index (NDVI) early time sequence. Few Haryana and Punjab districts were selected.
National Agriculture Imagery Program	During agricultural seasons in the United States, NAIP captures aerial imagery. Based on sufficient funds and the FSA imaging procurement process, NAIP programs are funded per year. NAIP imaging is collected with horizontal accuracy at a one-meter ground sample spacing (GSD) that fits the six-meter photo-identifiable field reference points utilized for a camera inspection.	(Wu et al., 2019)	The writers also developed a fully automatic solution to coastal flooding through Google Earth Computer. Machine study algorithms were used to classify aerial imagery with additional spectral indices, which were further refined with LiDAR-based depressions.
Sentinel-5P RTI/OFFL NRTI CLOUD	This dataset provides NRTI high-resolution imagery of cloud parameters.	(Griffin et al.)	The TROPOMI aerosol layer height commodity is here analyzed, with MISR and CALIOP observations in North America. Furthermore, device simulation studies were performed to explain the basic variations between the different goods. The findings demonstrate that MISR and TROPOMI are technically very similar to single-plum aerosol profiles.
Sentinel-5P RTI/OFFL Carbon Monoxide	This dataset includes high-resolution photographs of CO	(Korsunska et al., 2019)	A global assessment system has been developed

	concentrations nearly in real-time. The Sentinel 5 Precursor (S5P) satellite TROPOMI studies the global CO abundance, utilizing clear-sky and cloudy Earth radiance measurements within the 2,3µm Shortwave Infrared Spectrum (SWIR) band. Precise sky observations by TROPOMI have CO complete columns of tropospheric boundary awareness.		to determine quantitatively the success in meeting the sustainable development goals and how important success is. In this article, the writers suggest a method focused on harmonized satellite and in situ data to complete Air Quality (AQ) monitoring as part of the HORIZON 2020 initiative.
Sentinel-5P RTI/OFFL Ozone	This dataset provides NRTI high-resolution imagery of ozone concentrations.	(Hubert et al., 2019)	In this research article, the authors analyzed the quality of tropospheric ozone datasets derived from TROPOMI measurements of Sentinel-5.
Sentinel-5P RTI/OFFL Formaldehyde	This dataset includes high-resolution images of ambient formaldehyde concentrations (HCHO) in almost real-time.	(Omrani et al., 2020)	Air emission control is an important public safety activity. Data access is also hampered by the absence of the land surveillance network. Here the authors present a new space-time dataset, which has been collected and processed from the remote sensing platform Sentinel 5P. The authors used the complete workflow for the processing of nitrogen dioxide (NO2) measurements obtained from May 2018 to June 2019 across mainland France as an example.
Sentinel-2 Multispectral Instrument	This dataset is a multi-spectral, broad sweep project in support of Copernicus Land Monitoring projects, which involve habitat, soil and water cover mapping, inland rivers, and coastal areas surveillance. We were determined with sen2cor.	(Mahdianpari et al., 2019)	The first comprehensive distribution chart of one of the wealthiest regions of Canada for wetlands is provided in this report, covering approximately 106,000 square kilometres.
Sentinel-5P RTI/OFFL Sulphur Dioxide	This dataset provides nearly real-time high-resolution photographs of concentrations of ambient Sulphur dioxide (SO_2).	(Theys et al., 2017)	This paper introduces the vertical sulfur dioxide (SO2) column recovery algorithm implemented in the UPAS (UV/VIS Atmospheric Spectrometer Universal System) S-5P operational device and

			discusses its numerous recovery measures.
Sentinel-5P Aerosol Index	Its dataset contains high-resolution NRTI UV-aerosol (UVAI) images, often referred to as the Aerosol Absorption Index (AAI). The UV Aerosol Index is an indicator that measures the presence of aerosols that accumulate UV-like particles and soot. The UV Aerosol Index (AI) is a spectral comparison tool in an environment of UV with low ozone absorption.	(Ahn et al., 2018)	The TROPOMI AI software of ESA newly published can be linked to OMPS measurements using an updated algorithm. The latest AI derivation method has increased simulation ability for cloud dispersal using Mie theory and provides the influence of wavelength and angular surface reflection. An initial NASA TROPOMI Aerosol Algorithm (TROPOMAER) finding will be seen, which not only generates AI but also recovered aerosol optical depth products and a single albedo scatter.
Sentinel-3 OLCIEFR	The full resolution (EFR) Earth observation dataset of Ocean and Land Color Instrument (OLCI) contains top-level atmospheric radiations at 300 m, world-wide, every ~2 days. OLCI is one of the instruments for calculating oil colour, with high-end precision and reliability for supporting ocean forecast systems, and for environmental and climate monitoring, in the ESA/EUMETSAT Sentinel-3 Project.	(Uzhinskiy et al., 2018)	Throughout our work, the writers have attempted to forecast heavy metal air emissions by integrating satellite photos with machine learning. Product research datasets have been satellite photos from Google's Earth Engine software and sampling results from the UNECE International Cooperative Program (ICP) Vegetation's Data Management Network. The writers obtained good performance in the Norway Sb and Serbia Mn projection.
Sentinel-1 SAR GRD	This dataset provides ground-range detected scenes. Each scene has a resolution of 40, 25, or 10 m resolution.	(Rutkowski et al., 2018)	This paper introduces the specification for Sentinel-1 datasets of a newly built sequential shift detection algorithm focused on a likelihood ratio statistical omnibus on the Google Earth Engine framework. New monitoring strategies like the one illustrated here provide the nuclear non-proliferation community

			with a modern approach to track nuclear plants around the world through remote sensing datasets.
Sentinel-5P RTI/OFFL Nitrogen Dioxide	This dataset includes high-resolution measurements of NO$_2$ concentrations in near-real-time.	(Zheng et al., 2019)	The spatial-time characteristics and effect factors in mainland China for the troposphere NO2 column concentration in the year (February 2018 to January 2019) were first evaluated at two administrative rates to expose a condition of NO2 (based on the new Sentinel-5P TROPOMI NO2 products). Results indicate the obvious features "extreme in the winter and small in the summer" of the monthly floating column of tropospheric NO2, while the spatial distribution is a "strong in the east and small in the west" trend, bordered by the Hu axis.
Normalized Difference Water Index	This dataset provides the Normalized Difference Water Index, which represents the change water content of vegetation canopy.	(Tang et al., 2016)	The goal of this analysis was to create an acceptable index for Landsat images to chart the flood condition in Playa between March and April 1985–2015. To identify the plain flood conditions in Landsat images, four forms of spectral indices non-standardized vegetation index, Normalizing Water Difference Index (NDWI), adjusted NDWI, and Tasseled Cap Wetness-Greenness differential (TCWGD).
Normalized/Enhanced Vegetation Index	EVI is generating from each scene's close-IR, red and blue lines, varying between -1.0 and 1.0. This product comes from the surface reflectance composites MODIS/006/MOD09GA.	(Alonso et al., 2016)	The writers explain the preparation and interpretation measures to make some other case study feasible. After identifying the study area boundary, each consumer may construct a list and video of accessible Landsat or MODIS

			images, NDVI charts, and timescales of spatially applied NDVI values across the study area or a set of previously delineated polygons. Some of the difficulties the authors face is to differentiate between the various picture collections used for vegetation mapping in the GEE catalog. The authors review and compare the outcomes of five selected picture collections from Landsat and MODIS, and classify the collections that provide the best quality outcomes for our case study.
Normalized Burn Ratio Thermal	This dataset provides Normalized Burn Ratio Thermal produced from Near-Infrared band and Mid Infrared Band at 2215nm.	(Bastarrika et al., 2018)	A contrast of the automated approach with manually collected burned perimeters was found to be highly effective in 40 validation locations. Combined commission and omission burned type errors have been found below 20%. The most challenging places were the low time resolution of the sensor and the cloud cover persistence and uncertainty with croplands, especially in relation to commission errors.
USGS Landsat TOA Reflectance	These datasets provide top of atmospheric reflectance, and coefficients were derived from image metadata.	(Flood, 2014)	This essay provides significant analysis of the variations in the Australian landscape between ETM+ and OLI. The study is carried out with a view to both high-atmosphere reflectance, surface reflectance, and biophysical parameters from the corresponding reflectance spectrums. The findings indicate minor variations between sensors, which can be increased to a biophysical

			parameter through simulation.
USGS Landsat TM Collection	This dataset provides satellite imagery collection of Landsat scenes with the highest data quality.	(Chavez Jr, 1986)	This analysis digitally merged two sets of data with somewhat different features and created a single collection of data containing details from both sets. For their spectral details, Landsat Thematic Mapper (TM) data were chosen, and for primary information, a digitized panchromatic image was obtained as part of the National High-Altitude System (NHAP) in approximately 4-meter resolution.
Landsat Gross/Net Primary Production	This dataset provides gross primary production derived from reflectance of the surface, GPP presents carbon amount captured by ecosystem plants.	(Jay et al., 2016)	The authors tested a modern picture fusion methodology to use high-resolution Landsat ground cover data in an updated variant of the model of the CASA ecosystem to improve estimations of net primary output for continental United States terrestrial ecosystems.
Normalized Difference Snow Index	This dataset is used for the identification of snow through its characteristics. NDSI is measured with a spectrum of -1.0 to 1.0, utilizing green and mid-IR bands.	(Choi and Bindschadler, 2004)	This paper introduces a new algorithm built-in visible satellite and infrared imagery of ice sheets to detect clouds. The method detects potential cloud pixels by utilizing the normal snow differential index (NDSI). Possible cloud pixels will be formed into regions, and edges will be calculated.
Burn Area Index	This dataset provided a Burn Area Index generated from near-infrared and mid-infrared index and identified through the charcoal signal.	(Pereira, 2003)	In this article, the authors reviewed difficult aspects related to fire in savannas in the context of identification and mapping of burned areas.
USGS Landsat Raw Scenes	Tier 2 is allocated scenes that do not follow the Tier 1 requirements during production. The RMSE and other properties are evaluated by consumers	Nil	Nil

	involved in Tier 2 scenes to assess their suitability for usage in specific apps and studies.		
USGS Landsat MSS Collection	This dataset provides satellite imagery collection of Landsat scenes with the highest data quality. Tier 1 contains data processed by Level-1 Precision Terrain (L1TP) with well-defined radiometry and inter-calibrated through numerous sensors of Landsat.	(Khorram et al., 1987)	A stratification system was applied to the TM data focused on principal component analysis, classifying the data into 10 types of land use/landscape used to interpret the MSS results. Comparison of photo-interpreted land-use forms with Landsat land-use related styles reveals that TM results are far more reliable than the MSS results.
Landsat Global Land Surveys	The 1975 Global Land Survey (GLS) is a regional map series from the Landsat Multispectral Scanner (MSS). In 1972-1983, Landsat acquired most of the scenes 1-3. There have been several differences in Landsat 1-3 evidence in scenes obtained by Landsat 4-5 in 1982-1987. These data have four spectral bands: Green, Red, NIR, and SWIR. The pictures look red in the traditional False-color display, while the NIR unit, while red, shows foliage.	(Gutman et al., 2013)	This research tests the GLS datasets on their geographical range, time constancy, geodetic precision, continuity in radiometric validation, picture completeness, the extent of cloud interference, and remaining deficiencies.
USGS Landsat Surface Reflectance	This dataset contains satellite reflectance imagery of the surface. These pictures consist of five VNIR belts, two SWIR belts that are processed for surface reflectance, and two TIR (thermal infrared) belts that are processed for an orthorexia luminosity temperature. These data have been corrected atmospherically using LaSRC and include a CFMASK-generated cloud, shadow, water, and snow mask, together with a saturation mask per pixel.	(Yu et al., 2018b)	In this paper, the authors offered a way to use the GlobeLand30 (GLC30) products of 2000 and 2010, rather than manually marking field samples for 2005 in our study area, Bangladesh, on Google Earth Engine (GEE). Randomly produced samples from GlobeLand30 items are tested for accuracy, and the overall accuracy is approximately 84,8%.

3.7   Geospatial Data Analysis in Google Earth Engine

Some of the major issues confronting us today are the processing, interpretation, and analysis of data. There have been major challenges in coping with large datasets or a lengthy observing duration, such as pattern identification, geophysical tracking, and detection of unusual occurrences (natural hazards). The main challenges with these situations are how the seas with accessible knowledge will be accessed, analyzed, and visualized. Machine learning (ML), which involves numerous software artificial neural networks (ANN) and SVM (Support Vector Machines), is an important method for intelligent data interpretation, manipulation, and simulation in both geo and setting.

3.7.1 Machine Learning for Geospatial Data

First, let us consider the usual characteristics of geospatial anomalies and environmental data: non-linearity (linear models have minimal applicability); spatial and temporal non-stationarity, i.e., in many situations, the hypothesis of Spatio-temporal stationarity (second-order stationarity, core hypotheses) cannot be accepted; Such characteristics contradict conventional system implementations (including many geostatistical models) and render the study, simulation and visualization of geostatistical and environmental data quite difficult. As described above, the problems of several actual circumstances can be addressed in high-dimensional spaces (geo-features) (very frequently, this space has more than 10 dimensions). It contains original geographic space and various features originating from experimental models or other knowledge outlets, such as remote sensing images, slopes, or curvatures. They are centered on automated shifting templates. In the above situation, conventional (geo)statistical structures are either too complex for use or cannot be implemented. For example, the various graph can be used efficiently in less than 3 dimensions. Critical spatial and temporal data analysis and modeling (including forecasts and forecasting) problems, therefore, answer the development and implementation of data-sensitive, nonlinear, stable, and multivariate models running at large dimensions and having excellent generalizing characteristics. One possible solution can be based on the artificial neural networking model of the various architectures and philosophy of statistical learning (e.g., methods based on kernel: Vector Support Machines and Vector Regression Support). Let us note that these methods are strongly reliant on data quality and quantity (black/grey boxes). Therefore, various statistical/geostatistical methods are valuable and essential to monitor ML data processing and modeling efficiency. Vario-graph, for example, allows us to explain and model anisotropic spatial relationships, geographic patterns, local fluctuations, and noise rates.

3.7.2 Google Earth Engine and Machine Learning

Google Earth Engine integrates a multi-petabyte database of geospatial and satellite images with an interpretation application on a global scale. It makes scientific analysis and visualization of geospatial datasets available to detect changes, map trends, and quantify Earth's differences. Earth Engine collects, organizes, and provides satellite imagery for global data mining. The public data collection contains more than 40 years of historical Earth images, and new pictures are taken every day. Also, Earth Engine offers JavaScript and Python APIs as well as other resources that enable massive datasets to be analyzed. The time-lapse of the Google Earth Engine allows natural observations to understand and understand how the Earth's surface has been affected by various events and decisions for growth in the last 32 years. Many parts around the planet may be chosen to see the earth's adjustments rapidly and conveniently.

Figure 9 displays algorithms for data processing that are accessible on the Google Earth Engine platform. Google Earth Engine data processing framework facilitates deep learning/data mining detection and clustering methods for geospatial data analysis. Classification is the most significant and most widely employed data mining methodology. It is a process of finding a set of models which represent and distinguish data classes or concepts. The model extracted may be represented in different ways, such as the IF-THEN law, decision tree, and neural networking.

The clustering idea has been used for a long time. It has many uses, particularly in the sense of information retrieval and web services organization. The clustering's main aim is to locate information and locate the most relevant electronic resources in the current context. The clustering work ultimately contributed to the automated indexing of index and online documents. Clustering is a process in which we create a cluster of artifacts in which characteristics are somewhat identical. The clustering tries to store related information. Clustering is often associated with sorting, but the two vary. Objects are allocated in the grouping to predefined groups, while groups are created in the clustering phase. Also, the word "sex" is sometimes used:

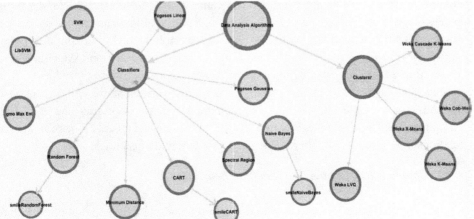

Figure 9 Google Earth Engine Data Analysis Algorithms Visualization in Gephi

3.8 GEE Data Analysis Algorithms Literature Survey

Geospatial data processing has numerous socioeconomic consequences, as well as geospatial data research used to address other societal problems. Table 6 provides a summary of the Google Earth Engine data analytics algorithms. The social implications of such algorithms are often discussed in the context of a literature study. The research papers which included data analysis/mining on geospatial data, which are also available in the Google Earth Engine, were chosen.

Table 6 GEE Data Analysis Algorithms with Social Implications

Algorithm Name	Machine Learning Technique	Algorithm Description	Authors	Social Implication/ Article Summary
Support Vector Machine (SVM)	Classification	SVM using a hyperplane to divide data into two groups. SVM executes a function identical to C4.5 at a large level except that SVM does not have decision-making bodies. A hyperplane is like a line equation, y = mx + b. Also, the hyperplane can be a line for a simple classification function with only two elements.	(Pourghasemi et al., 2013)	The analysis aims to generate a land susceptibility map using a GIS-based vector support machine (SVM) in Golestan province, Iran, Kalaleh Township. The landslide susceptibility indices were determined by using six forms of kernel feature classifiers using the help vector machine.
Pegasos Linear	Classification	Pegasos is a state of the art linear SVM solver, which uses a broad, multi-class model utilizing Stochastic Gradient Descent. Each class is allocated one single hyperplane (weight), and Pegasos predicts the most significant prediction dependent on the corresponding weight level.	(Padarian et al., 2015)	In these articles, the authors discuss how the Google Earth Engine automated soil mapping tool can be utilized by providing two instances of soil mapping in the neighbouring United States. The writers would also speak about the advantages and disadvantages of this application at the current implementation stage and future changes for a completely functioning soil mapping framework in the cloud.
Pegasos Gaussian	Classification	Pegasos Gaussian is a non-linear variant of the support vector machine. This algorithm uses the kernel of Gaussian. Optimization problems can be solved by using the Pegasos Gaussian algorithm; this algorithm utilized the Stochastic Gradient method.	Nil	Nil
Naïve Bayes	Classification	This algorithm applies the Bayesian theorem technique	(Lee et al., 2016)	1. The author demonstrates the usage of GEE to detect

		and is particularly suitable when the inputs' dimensions are small. Naive Bayes will also outperform more advanced classification approaches, given its simplicity. A variety of independent variables, whether constant or categorical, may be interpreted by Naive Bayes classifiers.	(Yalew et al., 2016a)	commercial palm oil plantations in Tripa, Aceh, Indonesia. Our Landsat 8 picture categorized ground cover with various spectral bands (RGB, NIR, SWIR, TIR, all classes) to differentiate land cover classification. 2. A web-based architecture (Agri-Suit) is created and presented, which integrates multiple global data from numerous sources for a multi-criteria agricultural land suitability evaluation on the platform of Google Earth Engine (GEE).
CART	Classification	CART decision Tree is a recursive partitioning method. CART is a conditional decision tree separating each of the input nodes into two children's nodes. The algorithm defines a condition at each stage of the decision tree – which variable and stage are to be used to divide the input node (data sample) into three children nodes.	(Patel et al., 2015)	In this article, the authors utilized the Google Earth Engine cloud computing platform and Landsat imagery to identify automatically urban areas by using the CART classification algorithm.
Spectral Region	Classification	Creates a classifier to check the inputs of a polygon inside an arbitrary 2D coordinate scheme described by a sequence of coordinates. Data to be graded should have two values (for example, pictures should have two bands). The outcome is one anywhere the input values are in the specified polygon, and 0.	Nil	Nil
Random Forest	Classification	Random forest algorithm is a randomized method for classification. This method, as the name implies, generates the forest with several leaves. Typically speaking, the more plants, the forest seems sturdy. Similarly, increasing the number of trees in the area, the higher the random forest ranking.	(Teluguntla et al., 2018) (Midekisa et al., 2017)	1. In this research study, authors utilized Google Earth Engine cloud computing platform Landsat imagery to accurately map cropland extent, and the Random Forest classifier was used to separate cropland and non-cropland area. 2. In this article, the authors utilized the Google Earth Engine cloud computing platform and Landsat imagery to measure the quantity of land

				cover and impervious land cover changes.
Minimum Distance Classifier	Classification	The minimal distance distinction is used to assign uncertain picture data into groups and reduce the difference between picture data and class in multi-functional environments. The distance is defined as a similarity index, such that the minimum distance is the same as the maximum similitude.	(Nikraftar et al., 2019)	The goal of this analysis is to generate landslide sensitivity maps in NI using three learning algorithms, including KNN, SVM, and RF. Overall 1334 landslides reported in the field of analysis 894 (altogether 67%), while the remaining 440 (altogether 33%) cases were used for the model validation.
GMO Max Entropy	Classification	The Max Entropy classification is a probabilistic classification, which belongs to the exponential models grouping. The Max Entropy does not presume that the functions are separate. The MaxEnt is focused on the concept of maximum entropy and selects the one with the most important entropy from all models which match our training results.	2017) (Shelestov et al., 2017)	This paper's key aim was to analyze pixel-based solutions to crop mapping in Ukraine and investigate the analysis ability of the GEE cloud framework to resolve the big data question and provide crop classification chart for vast regions.
Decision Tree	Classification	A decision tree is a classification algorithm. A prediction model or classification tree is generated via splitting a root node into sub-nodes. It is used for classification and regression problems.	(Zurqani et al., 2018) (Johansen et al., 2015)	1. In this article, the authors utilized the Google Earth Engine cloud computing platform to identify land cover classes in Savannah and also identify land cover temporal and spatial changes. 2. In this research article, the authors utilized the Google Earth Engine platform to identify a decrease in woody vegetation through the use of Landsat imagery in the state of Queensland, Australia.
Cascade K-Means	Clustering	Cascade K-Means clustering produced a k-set of disjoint clusters having common characteristics, and clusters are generated on training instances. The strongest K, according to calinski-harabasz criteria, is chosen in this algorithm.	(Vaz et al., 2019)	The writers here examine the Spatio-temporal contributions of non-native trees to the beauty of nature and natural activity in Portugal's national park. The scientists use a multimodal system to explain the environmental history and landscape visual-sensory components (colour variation, habitat biodiversity, and functionality of vegetation).
Weka CobWeb	Clustering	Weka CobWeb produces a clustering dendrogram similar	(Elias, 2003)	The authors concentrate on a method of deriving

		to a classification tree, distinguished by a probabilistic definition of each cluster. Cobweb produces hierarchical clustering, which probabilistically defines clusters. COBWEB uses heuristic assessment measures known as the category utility to guide tree building.		functionality from current spatial datasets automatically. It is a modern methodology to study current Space Databases and to attempt to automatically retrieve landmarks using the techniques of information exploration and data mining.
Weka K-Means	Clustering	Weka K-Means clustering produced a k-set of disjoint clusters having common characteristics; clusters are generated on training instances. It partitions the data space into cells of Verona.	(Mandal et al., 2018)	The method suggested is used to track different rice cultivars in three districts of the State of West Bengal, one of Indian's main rice-growing regions. The classification's consistency is tested at 150 validity points for the 2017 mountain season, including several lines.
Weka LVQ	Clustering	The LVQ combines vector quantization concepts and the nearest classification to update cluster centres at better recognition rates. In particular, LVQ is slowly upgrading the cluster centres so that modified centres can result in improved recognition accuracy.	(Mondal et al., 2018)	The authors using state-of-the-art Landsat technology. The cloud computing technologies to calculate Spatio-temporal shifts in land cover with an emphasis on mangrove habitats. The authors focused on a k-mean method for an unregulated classification and validated the categorized 2016 map using data from Sentinel-2 imagery.
Weka X-Means	Clustering	X-Means is K-Means expanded by a section of this aspect of the algorithm where the centres of their area are attempted to break. The decision was made by the children of each centre and themselves to equate the BIC principles of the two systems.	(Chandola et al., 2011)	The iGlobe framework is the desktop-based visualization and analytics platform for the smooth convergence of various geospatial datasets from several sources. It provides an interface for immersive review of the different datasets and almost real-time implementation of advanced data processing and mining algorithms.

3.9 Combined Data Analysis on Google Earth Engine Platform

3.9.1 SCENARIO-I

Machine learning algorithms can be used for data analysis purposes on Google Earth Engine Datasets. Google Earth Engine code editor provides many machine learning classifications and clustering algorithms for data analysis purposes; some of these datasets are naïve Bayes, decision tree, Random Forest, and Weka Cascade KMeans. Data Analysis on multiple kinds of Google Earth Engine datasets can help us derive the ratio of the crop production area of study and future prediction of permanent drought on land through analysis of multiple JRC Monthly Water History and Global Tera Land Surface temperature datasets. Combine data analysis on a different kind of Google Earth Engine Datasets is logical, based on such kind of data analysis decisions can be made to estimate future demand and supply of crops. Some future vegetation changes that probably could arise in particular land can be predicted earlier.

In Figure 10, PDSI refers to the "University of Idaho Palmer Drought Severity Index" dataset, this dataset is a globally measurement of soil dryness based on temperature and recent precipitation. JRC Monthly Water History, v1.1 in GEE, is a global collection of land water detection on month by month essential present from since 1984. MOD11A1.006 refers to the "Terra Land Surface Temperature and Emissivity Daily Global 1km dataset", this dataset emissivity and daily land surface temperature globally. GFSAD1000 refers to "Cropland Extent 1km Crop Dominance, Global Food-Support Analysis Data", this dataset provides the spatial distribution of significant cropland types (soybeans, rice, wheat, barley, corn). After a combined analysis of PDSI, JRC, MOD11A1.006, and GFSAD1000 datasets by using machine learning algorithms, one can predict the future growth of crop growth in specific cropland and could estimate the future vegetation changes in cropland. Growth of crops depends on water, soil moisture, and land temperature; all of these factors can be calculated through datasets as mentioned earlier. Earlier prediction of crop growth or production would help tackle the food crisis and manage or estimate demand and supply of food. Further, combined analysis of datasets, as mentioned earlier, could help in determining or predict chances whether to be under consideration; land could face permanent drought situations soon. Most of the reasons for drought are low land water, temperature, and yearly precipitation amount; having these factors historical data available, one could easily predict the chances of specific land permanent drought situation through data analysis.

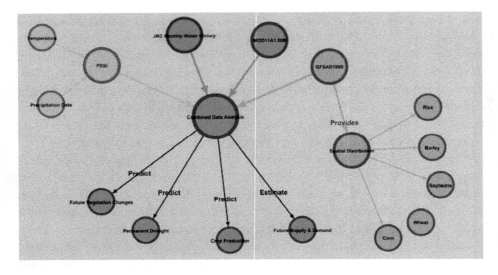

Figure 10 Combined Analysis of GEE datasets

3.9.2 SCENARIO-II

Figure 10 shows that Fruits and vegetables are growing and inexpensive vitamins and minerals sources. These are normal human diet components. The rising idea of the 'Healthy Diet' is also increasing regularly. Concentrations of toxic gasses in the air, on the other hand, are also growing due to increasing population and road traffic. These toxic gasses affect not only human health but also harm fruit and vegetable growth and freshness. In low environmental conditions, specific air emissions constantly kill crops and plants, and most plants lose their leaves before their maximum development due to polluted pollution. Google Earth Engine offers many datasets focused on an interpretation of such datasets, for evaluating the suitability of vegetation property, the potential air quality of particular soil may be predicted. Sentinel-5P NRTI O3 refers to the 'near real-time ozone dataset,' this dataset presents ozone (03) concentration in the air; ozone levels in the air are one of the most important reasons behind smog in summer. In summer. In Figure 11, Sentinel-5P, NRTI NO2 refers to the 'Near Real-Time Nitrogen Dioxide Dataset,' which maps the nitrogen dioxide layer on selected soils. Additional Nitrogen Dioxide availabilities of selected soil can be determined from the layer plotted. Sentinel-5P NRTI SO2 map virtually exact concentrations layer of sulfur dioxide on selected land. Sentinel-5P NRTI CO map almost real-time concentrations layer of carbon monoxide on the select ground.

Lack of toxic air mainly contains nitrogen dioxide, carbon monoxide, sulfur dioxide, and ozone concentrations available. The above datasets can be found in the Google

Earth Engine Data Catalog. After a combined data sample analysis, as stated earlier, the future air quality of any specific soil may easily be predicted or created, as detection of air quality contributes to the option of whether or not the specific air quality is appropriate for vegetation or agriculture. Many vegetables are vulnerable to air emissions, for example, Beans, broccoli, onion, cabbage, radish, spinach, corn nice, pepper, mouthwatering. Therefore, in every land recognition of air quality, it is a must for the fresh or safe development of vegetables. The projected growth ratio of every crop form on a given soil, based on datasets research, can also be identified with future air quality prediction. It would enable farm divisions or managers to take the appropriate action early to ensure that citizens on the land have access to a certain crop form. As well as an agricultural strategy, machine learning study of Sentinel-5P NRTI NO2, Sentinel-5P NRTI Co-Sentinel-5P NRTI SO2 datasets will also assist the nation, private land developers, or housing agencies in evaluating potential air quality of the land under consideration for human habitat safety in the earlier planning process before de Sentinel-5P NRTI NO2. It will be an economical way to assess air quality using Google Earth Engine datasets readily available. European Union/ESA/Copernicus programs and Sentinel-5 Precursor are the satellite deployed by the European Space Agency to control air quality on 13 October 2017. The onboard system is also named Tropomi (TROPOspheric Monitoring Instrument).

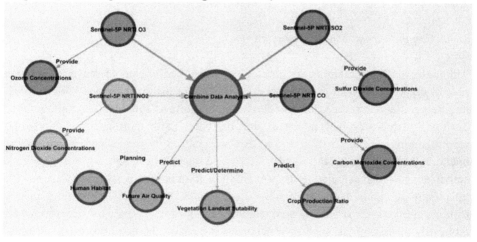

Figure 11 Sentinel-5 Datasets Combined Analysis for Determining Air Quality

3.10 Challenges and Future Work

One of the benefits of using the Earth Engine is that the consumer is almost fully isolated from operating information in parallel processing environments. Almost all facets of measurement management, including resource sharing, parallelism, data delivery, and retrieval, are managed and hidden. Such actions are solely procedural, so none of them may impact even the length of a demand. The price of freedom from this knowledge is that the consumer is powerless to control it: it is solely the machine that determines whether to execute a calculation. It contributes to some interesting problems in both device architecture and application.

3.10.1 Scaling challenges

The Earth Engine network will perform detailed calculations, but essentially the fundamental framework is a collection of low-end servers. There is not an alternative in this setting to install huge computers, and there is a strict cap on the amount of data that can be transmitted to each computer. It implies users can use the parallel processing primitives in the Earth Engine Library only to communicate broad calculations. It is practically impractical to successfully carry out other non-parallelizable operations in this setting. The need to communicate computations via the Earth Engine library often requires transforming current algorithms and workflows for the usage of the Earth Engine API to use the Earth Engine API. Because Earth Engine is a popular computer tool, restrictions, and other protections are required to prevent users from monopolizing the network.

3.10.2 Computational Model Mismatch

Although parallel operations are commonly distributed in remote sensing, there are several other operational groups that are not parallel or not accommodated in Earth Engine parallel computing constructions. The platform is suitable for neighbourhood operations with a per-pixel and finite value, like bands math, morphological operations, spectral unmixing, sample matching and texture analysis, as well as long chains of these operations (hundreds to thousands). It is also highly designed for computational activities, such as calculating information on a time series stack of images and effectively accommodating incredibly dense stacks, which are millions of images, trillions of pixels, for streaming applications. This does not operate for operations with arbitrarily distant inputs, such as watershed analyzer or classic clustering algorithms, where a local value may be determined by a large number of results, such as training a large number of conventional machine learning models, and operations requiring lengthy iterative processes such as finite element analysis or Also, data-intensive models which involve large data volumes not already available in Earth Engine may require considerable additional effort. These code methods can still be used in Earth Engine but also with strict limits of scaling.

3.10.3 Client/Server Programming Model

Users of the Earth Engine are still ignorant of the concept of client-server programming. The libraries in Earth Engine clients aim to include a recognizable procedural programming context, but this may contribute to frustration where the user ignores the calculation itself is not performed by their local programming environment (for example, a Python script). The whole chain is registered and transmitted to the server for execution via customer proxy objects, so this ensures that Earth Engine database calls cannot be combined with normal local computing idioms. It contains some basic language features such as conditionals and loops that depend on calculated values and standard numerical packages. Users may also use these external devices, but they cannot explicitly add them to Earth Engine proxy artefacts, occasionally creating uncertainty.

3.10.4 Advancing the State of the Art

Earth Engine's ultimate objective is to enable progress on humanity's biggest problems while making it possible to control, map, and maintain the climate and energy. It includes exposure to not only unnecessary data and computing resources but also increasingly specialized analytical methods that are simple to use. To that end, the integration of deep learning techniques, TensorFlow, Reinforcement Learning Techniques, and other scalable infrastructures, including the Google Compute Engine and BigQuery, are ongoing experiments.

3.11 Data Collection Process

3.11.1 Study Area

The research field for this analysis was Pakistan, which is considered the world's largest cropland region. Further stratified Pakistani regions into four RAEZs helped classify the areas with common cultivation, soil types and environmental trends, and the developed Agroecological areas Figure 12. The adjustments in the regional Agro-ecologic zones (GAEZs) of the Food and Agriculture Organization (FAOs) dependent on the amounts of days, soil and field data collected in 10 km, are the RAEZs. GAEZs, though, have too many regions to be graded because many of these regions have only very low amounts of agriculture compared to the total region of the city. Consequently, we have optimized GAEZ to RAEZs by the usage of the ASTER global optical radiometer (V2) 30-m (30 m GDEM) and the proportion of cultivated land in a field by utilizing Advanced Spatial Thermal Emission & Reflection (ASTER) data slope. A variety of smaller RAEZs have been merged into broader areas based on the region's cropland value.

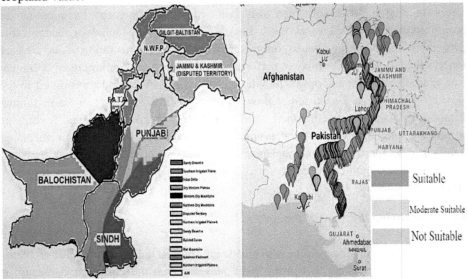

Figure 12 Stratification of the field of research into specific, large defined Agro-ecological areas (RAEZs). This chart demonstrates also the distribution of the reference training data used in algorithms for machine learning. The machine-learning algorithms use

3.11.2 Datasets

The following datasets were utilized in this research study to produce a prediction model for assessing agricultural land suitability. First, different datasets that were utilized in this research study are described and discussed below followed by reference training and validation data of Pakistan.

- NASA-USDA SMAP Global Soil Moisture Data
- SRTM Digital Elevation Data 30m
- ERA5 Monthly aggregates
- OpenLandMap Soil texture class (USDA system)
- Keetch-Byram Drought Index
- OpenLandMap Soil pH in H2O
- MCD15A3H.006 MODIS Leaf Area Index/FPAR 4-Day Global 500m

3.11.2.1   NASA-USDA SMAP Global Soil Moisture Data

NASA-USDA Global Soil Humidity and NASA-USDA SMAP global soil humidity data sets have world-wide soil humidity knowledge at a spatial resolution of 0.25°x0.25°. Such databases involve soil and surface humidity (mm), soil humidity percentage, and soil surface and air moisture anomalies. Soil moisture is a crucial element in regulating the flow between the soil and the environment of water and heat energy by evaporation and plants' transpiration. As a consequence, soil humidity plays a major role in environmental patterns and precipitation development.

3.11.2.2   SRTM Digital Elevation Data 30m

USGS Virtual elevation models (DEM) sequences frequently spaced elevation values linked horizontally to either a UTM or spatial coordinate system map. South to north profiles organized from West to East is uniformly distributed between the grid groups. Using the 3D Elevation System (3DEP), USGS acquires data for the origins of bare Earth elevation and re-examines data into many regional chart DEM items for the United States and regions. The DEM goods include 2, 1, 1/3 and 1/9 arc-second levels, 5 m DEMs in Alaska and 1 m in the restricted US. DEMs are also used in DEM goods. Across their respective geographical zones, the 2, 1, and 1:3 arc-second DEMs compose of logically smooth field surfaces and are constructed from best performing data in the USGS.

3.11.2.3   ERA5 Monthly aggregates

The primary factor that influences plant growth rate is temperature. Warmer conditions and potential for more severe weather occurrences are likely to affect the efficiency of the factory. Pollination constitutes one of the most vulnerable phenological processes to severe temperatures among all organisms, and extreme temperatures will have a direct effect on growth in this stage of progress. Of the seven ERA5 climate research criteria, the ERA5 MONTHLY offers composite values for several months: temperature of 2 m air, temperature 2 m dew-pointe, total precipitation, ambient water level, surface density, 10 m u-WC and 10 m v-WC. Therefore, the mean monthly and average air temperature is measured based on 2 m air temperature data per hour. Included in monthly numbers are cumulative precipitation levels. All other criteria are given on average per month.

3.11.2.4   OpenLandMap Soil texture class (USDA system)

The soil properties decide how easily water flows through saturated soil; the water flows through sandy soils more readily than across clay-like soils. The soil quality often determines the amount of water accessible for the plant after the field potential is reached; soils with clay are more water-supporting than sandy soils. Therefore, well-drained soils typically have strong soil aeration, ensuring it is air-like that allows a healthy growth of the root and therefore, a safe harvest. The soil with a large proportion of the silt and clay particles has a higher probability than a sandy surface in the same parameters. The surface has a smaller percentage of the silt and the clay particulates. Groups of soil texture (USDA system), at depths of 6 soils (0, 10, 30, 60, 100 and 200 cm), at 250 m from soil texture fractions, as foreseen, utilizing the R soil texture kit.

3.11.2.5   Keetch-Byram Drought Index

To order to determine future eruption, Keetch and Byram (1968) have developed a drought map. It reflects the combined impact of evapotranspiration and rainfall on deeper and upper soil layers causing accumulated humidity deficiency. It is a cumulative measure of organic content in the soil inflammability. The KBDI aims to calculate precipitation rates required to restore the planet to maximum field efficiency. The KBDI tries to quantify precipitation amounts. It is a closed device with a nominal range of 0 to 800 units and a humidity level in the soil of 0 to 8 inches. The KBDI expects saturation at 8 inches of vapour. None is the level of no shortage in precipitation and 800 is the highest potential drought. The index number shows the sum of net precipitation required to decrease the index to zero or saturation at each point on the graph. KBDI inputs are the latitude of the facility, average annual precipitation, cumulative dry bulb and the last 24 hours of precipitation. Drought decrease only happens when precipitation is greater than 0.20 "(referred to as net precipitation). Droughts rate is decreased by the total volume of rain and drought levels are raised by a measure of drought.

3.11.2.6   OpenLandMap Soil pH in H2O

The soil's pH will change over time, as factors such as parent material, weathering, and current farming practices change. It will fluctuate throughout the year as well. Soil pH is going to affect plants' cultivation. You have to consider the soil's acidity and recognize that the soil comprises various materials that decide its properties. They comprise mineral particles (sand, silt, colour, soil composition), organic matter (living and dead), and air and water. The pH is determined in the water portion where dissolved chemicals produce the acid or alkaline soil. The pH ranges from 0 (most acids) and 14 (most alkaline), and the pH range 7 (neutered). Soil acidity and alkalinity are calculated in units of pH. The pH scale and plant growth relation as shown in Figure 13 below.

pH Scale

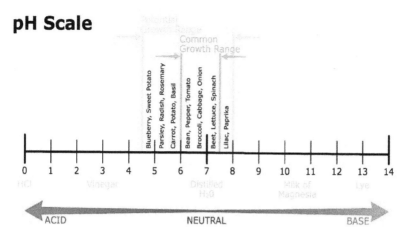

Figure 13 pH Scale and plant growth

3.11.2.7   MCD15A3H.006 MODIS Leaf Area Index

A significant parameter of plant ecology is the leaf area index (LAI). It is an indicator of the active photosynthetic zone and the region prone to transpiration simultaneously as it shows how much foil there is. This data set contains the index of the region of the leaf (LAI), and the component of photosynthetically active radiation (FPAR) received by plants from the BIR (BIR) Terra and Aqua. LAI and FPAR are the main parameters for modeling the movement between soil, environment and habitats of oil, water and carbon.

3.12 Satellite Imagery Composite Bands

GEE cloud-based databases alluded to in section 3.7.2 for two years (2018-2019) have been arranged for Pakistan to cover crop dynamics in various periods. There is a specific re-visiting period for each satellite, and because of the cloud scope, it is not feasible to acquire constant, wall-to-wall cloud-free time-series data for each area. Bicycle/trimester composites have been designed to overcome this restriction and guarantee cloud-free and nearly cloud-free wall-to-all visibility (depending on the countries/regions). Ultimately, the following measures lead to a 48-band MFDC Figure 14 for six time-periods (time composites), producing 10-m to 60-mega-file data-cubes.

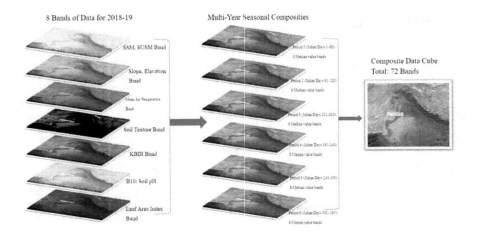

8 Bands of Data for 2018-19

SSM, SUSM Band

Slope, Elevation Band

Mean Air Temperature Band

Soil Texture Band

KBDI Band

B10: Soil pH

Leaf Area Index Band

Multi-Year Seasonal Composites

Period 1 (Julian Days 1-60)
9 Median value bands

Period 2 (Julian Days 61-120)
9 Median value bands

Period 3 (Julian Days 121-180)
9 Median value bands

Period 4 (Julian Days 181-240)
9 Median value bands

Period 5 (Julian Days 241-300)
9 Median value bands

Period 6 (Julian Days 301-365)
9 Median value bands

Composite Data Cube
Total: 72 Bands

Pakistan

Figure 14 Composite Data Cube in the period 2018–2019 with 6-time spans. Nine bands (composed of a median pixel throughout the period, with each day (e.g. day 1: Days 1 to 60 of Julian) resided in Google Earth Engine Catalogue with a 72,000 mega disk cube.

To: (1) ensure wall-to-wall coverage of data and (2) reduce the effects of cloud coverage, we used the multi-year (2018-2019) data. Based on the region's seasonal fluctuations and supply of cloud-free data, the 2018 and 2019 nominal years were split further into different cycles, or phases Figure 14. MFDC cloud-free wall-to-wall collections were built on a bi-monthly or tri-monthly basis Figure 14 in Pakistan. Cloud-free or nearly cloud-free photos for two-month time intervals may be produced Figure 14, which will include a total of 6 cycles (1 cycle of Julie's day from one to six; 2 duration from 1 July to sixty; 2 cycles from 61 to twenty years; 3 months from 121-180; 4 months from 181-240, 4 months from 241-300; 6:301-365; 3.9) for 12 months. It is worth mentioning that multi-year details (2018–2019) for each period (e.g. 1–60 days) is used to increase the chances of mere cloud pixels across Pakistan. With each time the following relations and indexes also apply soil-moisture level (25,39 mm), soil surface humidity (274,6 mm), slope (max: 25), height (-10-6500), average air temperature (224-304 K), the soil density, crop-drought index Keetch-Byram (0-800 max), H2o soil pH (42-110), leaf-area index (0-100) as shown in Figure 14. It culminated in a 72-band MFDC Figure 14 of nine median value strings, which were distributed over six time periods. The band stack and periods are leading to MFDC. Both compositions were carried out for planetary data processing on the GEE cloud-based geospatial network, as shown in Table 7.

Table 7 Characteristics of multi-temporal multi-year GEE data used in the study.

Country Name	Band Name	The Mega-File Data Cube with Total# Of Bands	The time-composited of Julian Days over data	Data of Years	The name of Data provider
Pakistan	Surface Soil Moisture (SSM)	72	C1: 1-60 C2: 61-120 C3: 121-180 C4: 181-240 C5: 241-300 C6: 301-365	2018, 2019	NASA GSFC
	Sub Surface Soil Moisture (SUSM)				
	Slope				NASA/USGS/JPL-Caltech
	Elevation				
	Mean Air Temperature				ECMWF/Copernicus Climate Change Service
	Soil Texture				envirometrix, openlandmap, opengeohub, soil, texture, usda
	Keetch–Byram drought index (KBDI)				Institute of Industrial Science, The University of Tokyo, Japan
	Soil pH in H2O				EnvirometriX Ltd
	Leaf Area Index				NASA LP DAAC at the USGS EROS Center

3.12.1 *Reference land surface samples for training and validation*

Table 8 includes a description of the sample distribution and validity results of the comparison study.

Table 8 Education and testing details for guides. Most test models are used in the training of algorithms for machine learning and the number of samples that are checked for independent precision assessment.

Country	Class	Training Samples	Validation Samples
Pakistan	Highly Suitable	1530	1200
	Moderate Suitable	1386	1000
	Not Suitable	2070	1500

Regarding Pakistan, comparison training and evaluation data were collected, and part of the training data was used to gather information and train the MLA. The precision, mistake and inconsistencies in testing results have been used to test them. In the sense of the cropland description, data were collected. In this analysis, croplands were described as farm fields with annual crops + cropland fallows + permanent crops. A wide variety of strongly suited and unsuited croplands and reasonably appropriate groups of crops with outstanding spatial distribution in Pakistan have been collected with samples Figure 15. Because satellite data for the 2018–2019-time cycle have been obtained, there is a risk that cropland in one year or season may appear to be cropland defective in the next year or year. Some images were collected from submeters to 10 meters of spatial imagery (VHRI) in Pakistan and some years of imagery from Google Earth Engine. We also obtained from this 4986 and 3700 samples of validation Figure 15.

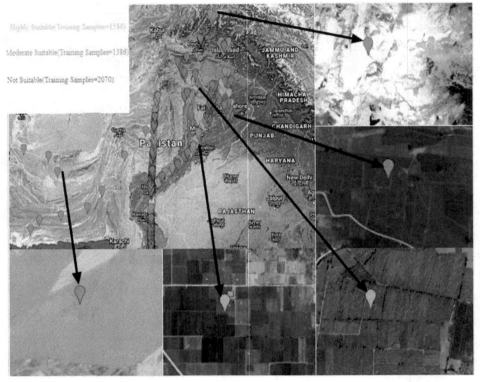

Figure 15 Sub metrical imagery details for Pakistan at 10 m, very high quality. Illustration of Pakistan's referral training data obtained utilizing a very high spatial resolution submeter at 10 m imaging.

3.12.2 Multi Decision Criteria for Labelling Reference Dataset

Training datasets are named based on the UN Food and Agriculture Organization (FAO) literary analysis and basic values. The following

Table 9 specifies multi-decision requirements for the marking of reference results.

Table 9 Different criteria used for land suitability classes

Suitability Criteria Type	Suitability Classes			Criteria Defined By
	Highly Suitable	**Moderate Suitable**	**Not Suitable**	
Surface Soil Moisture (ssm)	20-25mm	>15-20mm	<10mm	International Production Assessment Division
Sub Surface Soil Moisture (susm)	>68.75mm	<68.75mm	<17.0252	International Production Assessment Division
Slope	0-2m	>2m	>5m	(Yalew et al., 2016b)
Elevation	<=150m	150-250m	>250m	
Mean Air Temperature	288.15 K to 298.15 K	281.15 K to 287.15 K	< 281.15 K or > 304 K	(Aldababseh et al., 2018), (Karimi et al., 2018), International Production Assessment Division
Keetch–Byram drought index (KBDI)	0-400	401-600	601-800	Wildland Fire Assessment System
Soil pH in H2O (B10)	74-78	71-73 and 79-81	<71 and > 81	Department of Primary Industries and Regional Development, Government of Western Australia
Leaf Area Index (Lai)	>40	20-41	<20	(Otgonbayar et al., 2017)
Soil Texture (B10)	Inceptisols	Aridisols	Entisols	(Aymen et al., 2020)

3.12.3 *Reference Dataset Labelling Process*

The process of labeling training data points is shown in following Figure 16. As shown in the following Figure 16, the first study area was selected, which is Pakistan, in the next phase Google Earth Engine, several geospatial datasets were mapped on the selected study area. Details of Google Earth Engine datasets were provided in section 3.7.2. In the next step, the bands values of each reference data point were extracted and mapped against the multi-criteria, which were discussed in 3.8.2. Based on the criteria, the class of reference data was selected and labeled (e.g. Highly Suitable).

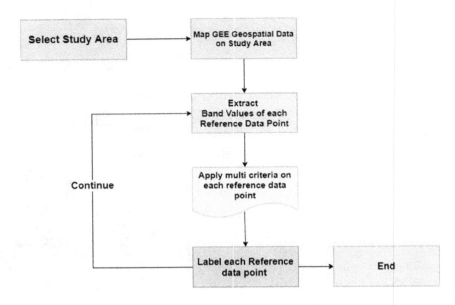

Figure 16 Labelling process of Training Datapoints

3.13 Research Methodology

In this study research process, as shown in Figure 17, first a thorough literature review and descriptive study were conducted on Google Erath Engine geo-environmental datasets related to climate, vegetation indexes, elevation, and so on. In the descriptive study of datasets, datasets' features or attributes were identified for analysis purposes at further stages of the research process. At the next stage, a literature review and descriptive study about different machine learning algorithms were conducted for extracting knowledge about the performance and applicability of machine learning algorithms on different data types perspective. The choice of machine learning algorithms and techniques was identified on datasets attributes and descriptive study, which was conducted at an earlier stage. Google Earth Engine provides several climates, water history, and vegetation indexes datasets of more than 20 years long, so the next step of this research study was collecting random training samples after mapping the respective dataset layer on the chosen land boundary. Training samples were taken under both cloudy or not cloudy environments, and collected samples also belonged from different years. Google Earth Engine also provides a cloud-based computation facility for the analysis of petabytes data. In the next phase, after a thorough study of both geo-environmental datasets and machine learning algorithms, chosen machine learning algorithms were applied on training datasets and the land suitability detection model was developed as a result. In this research study water history, toxic gasses in air, drought severity index of chosen land (Pakistan Agriculture Land) was visualized for getting an idea about what is going to happen in the near future related to the environment and land nutrition situation; this will help management to take earlier decision to prevent drought or some other worst scenarios. Land nutrition and atmosphere are important factors behind the healthy growth of plants and crops.

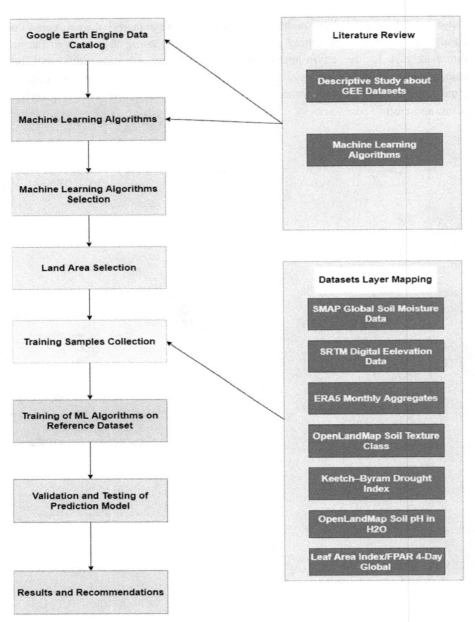

Figure 17 Methodology for Development of Land Suitability Prediction Mode

4   Results and Discussion

4.1   Agriculture Land Suitability Prediction Map for Pakistan

Under this segment, there are three separate components. It starts with a demonstration of the drug for Pakistan of the up to 60 meters of Sentinel-2 MSI. It includes an assessment of cropland distribution commodity precisions, mistakes, and uncertainties. Croplands are then described and addressed at a regional level.

4.2   10m to 60-m cropland extent product for Pakistan

In the nominal years 2018-2018, the trial generated 10 to 60 m of cropland, extracted from Sentinel-2 MSI 5-day time series data for Pakistan. The machine learning algorithms listed in section 4 were used to distinguish the croplands from the non-croplands in the GEE cloud computing setting. The method was iterated, and the samples were modified to the algorithms several times before optimum cultivable cropland outcomes relative to non-cropland were obtained.

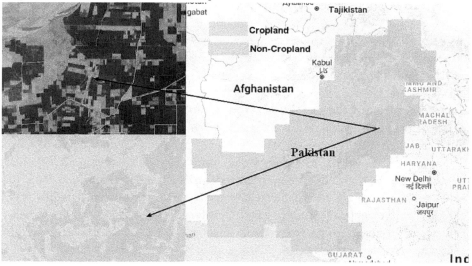

Table 10 A device with a view to a position (lower left) and corresponding high-resolution (upper left-hand side) at 10-m to 60-m for Pakistan (right-hand panel) with the illuminating zoom

4.3   The Assessment of Accuracy

The cropland map for Pakistan was evaluated for accuracy with an error matrix that did not apply to the manufacturer of this dataset (Congalton et al., 2017). For the entire world, the accuracy error matrix has been developed. The exactness of the ultimate cropland map of Pakistan was calculated using a minimum of 200 stratified, randomly spaced testing samples. An error matrix for complete accuracy (Pakistan as a whole), Naïve Bayes, Ride, Random Tree, and SVM algorithms have been developed, and its accuracy is provided below on a 10m to 60m Sentinel2 MSI dataset and validation data collection. The average precision of CART algorithm was 82%, with an accuracy of 89% of the producer, and 73.0% of the customer for cropland class. The validation data collection had complete accuracy of 75% for the Random Forest method, with vendor accuracy of 77% for cropland class and implementation accuracy of 71.0%. The validation data collection was 76% for the Naïve Bays method, 81% for the manufacture, and 54,0% for the cropland class for the consumer accuracy. Likewise, SVM's total validity data accuracy was 74%, and the producer's accuracy was 76%, while cropland accuracy was 68%. The performance of the algorithm CART with the best average validity performance relative to the other three algorithms.

Classification accuracies can be further increased-particularly the accuracies of the consumer and of the supplier. Second, by separating the regions. Google Earth Engine (GEE) is a powerful tool for capturing, storing and classifying photographs via a cloud storage network. While GEE allows handling large data and easily calculate, it is restricted to how GEE handles large data using MLAs. There are still several difficulties to overcome, such as the lack of data relating to comparative training from agricultural fields of greater variety. Back to Mail Online home. Back to the page, you came from e.g., for a certain classifier, the "study" of the entire broad data population contributes to inconsistencies in the classification performance and a decrease in accuracy, instead of classifying data for each pixel. Many directions to boost precision and rising uncertainty are better spatial mapping, such as the convergence of global forest maps (Hansen et al., 2013) and global water masks (Carroll et al., 2009). Since 10 m to 60 meters of Sentinel 2 images are thousands of pixels in such wide fields, this isn't a really large study, but maybe the best one to obtain, considering the difficulty of broad areas and capital. The larger samples for both training and testing are possible, particularly in numerous croplands, from highland to lowland deltas that take into consideration specific subspecies within permanent cultivations, cropland falls, and permanent plants. Identical approaches often accompanied many nations of the world to those employed here. In a recent report on Africa (Xiong et al., 2017c), for instance, 94% of the development lands had an average weighted precision (85% or 14.1% omission error) and 68.5% (31.5% commission error), with a producers accuracy of 85% and an Africa wide consumer accuracy (31.5% commission error) as shown in Table 11.

Table 11 The Computer analysis performance error matrix algorithms with 10 m to 60 m Cropland Expanded Commodity for Pakistan precision error matrix

CART Algorithm Accuracy on Training and Validation Dataset

	Cropland	Non- Cropland	Total	User Accuracy	Classification Accuracy: 93%
Cropland	73	27	100	73%	
Non- Cropland	9	91	100	91%	
Total	82	118	200		
Producer Accuracy	89%	77%			Validation Accuracy: 82%

Random Forest Algorithm Accuracy on Training and Validation Dataset

	Cropland	Non- Cropland	Total	User Accuracy	Classification Accuracy: 91%
Cropland	71	29	100	71%	
Non- Cropland	21	79	100	79%	
Total	92	108	200		
Producer Accuracy	77%	73%			Validation Accuracy: 75%

Naïve Bayes Algorithm Accuracy on Training and Validation Dataset

	Cropland	Non- Cropland	Total	User Accuracy	Classification Accuracy: 83%
Cropland	54	46	100	54%	
Non- Cropland	13	87	100	87%	
Total	67	133	200		
Producer Accuracy	81%	65%			Validation Accuracy: 76%

Support Vector Machine Algorithm Accuracy on Training and Validation Dataset

	Cropland	Non- Cropland	Total	User Accuracy	Classification Accuracy: 83%
Cropland	68	32	100	68%	
Non- Cropland	21	79	100	79%	
Total	89	111	200		
Producer Accuracy	76%	71%			Validation Accuracy: 74%

4.4 The Comparison with Statistics from Other Sources and Cropland Areas

Aside from creating a map, it is an essential component of the 10 to the 60-m region of cropland commodity to quantify the cropland region statistics. Pakistan has two distinct types of cropland (croplands and pastures under management). For the year 2018-2019, Pakistan's gross cropland region has been estimated at 370,200 square kilometers. The statistics for the cropland area produced for Pakistan from this study compared to other sources like the Pakistan Statistical Bureau. However, the area created by this analysis of the cultivated land in Pakistan between 10 m and 60 m is high. Every pixel up to 60-m is approximately 0.099 ha. Therefore, it is necessary, also at the farm stage, big or tiny, to catch regions at the sub-national level. It is a significant advantage compared to other cropland goods currently usable, as shown in Table 12.

Table 12 Net cropland areas derived based on 10-m to 60-m Sentinel-2 MSI

Country	Agriculture Land in Sq. Km (The World Bank Data)	Govt. of Pakistan (Agriculture Census Organization-2010) in Sq. Km.	Net Cropland Area in Sq. Km. (Estimated in Current Study)	Agriculture Land (Pakistan Bureau of Statistics) in Sq. Km.	% of Total Agriculture Land Areas
Pakistan	368,440	274,814	370,200	303,400	47.79%

4.5 Visualization of Air Quality

4.5.1 Near Real-Time Carbon Monoxide

Carbon monoxide is a poisonous gas produced typically by fossil fuels and induces growth processes in the soil due to its high strength. As seen in Figure 18, the northern areas of Pakistan have lower carbon monoxide rates in soil, and those of Punjab have lower levels of carbon monoxide, especially in the Lahore and Faisalabad regions. A study of the seasonal variations of Islamabad's air emissions, Karachi, Peshawar and Lahore shows higher rates of CO in winter. The available information from 2007 to 2010 has been investigated in Lahore, Peshawar and Peshawar (71 µg/m3), Karachi and Islamabad (61 µg/m3) (61 µg/m3) with a considerable quantity of fine particle material (PM 2.5).

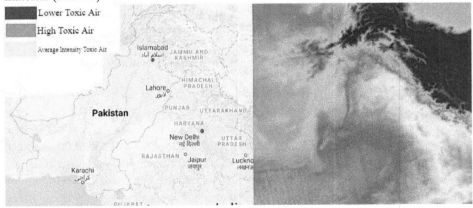

Figure 18 Near Real-Time Carbon Monoxide Visualization of Pakistan

4.5.2 Near Real-Time Nitrogen Dioxide

The nitrogen Dioxide content amount in Pakistan's air is illustrated in Figure 19; in short-term amounts of 120 µg/m3 nitrogen dioxide is poisonous to plants. The production of plants is decreased. The impacts on the environment become greater as sulfur dioxide and ozone both exist. Carbon dioxide can cause acid rain, along with sulfur dioxide. The 48-hour data show that the present levels in Pakistan are marginally

112

higher, compared to the WHO air quality guideline value of 40 µg/m3, based on annual concentrations of nitrogen dioxide (NO2). Peshawar (52 ± 21 µg/m3), Islamabad (49 ± 28 µg/m3), Lahore (49 ± 25 µg/m3), and Karachi (46 ± 15 µg/ m3) have become the most prevalent of concentrations. Quetta had slightly lower concentrations (37 ± 15 µg/m3).

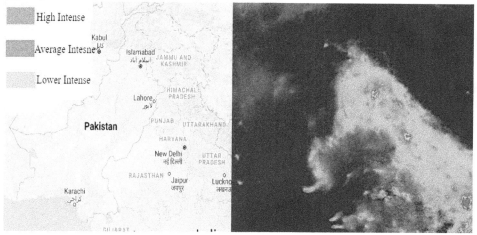

Figure 19 Near Real-Time Nitrogen Dioxide Visualization of Pakistan

4.6 Agriculture Suitable Areas and comparison with statistics from other sources

In addition to generating a map, it is an essential item in the research analysis that the cropland areas' figures are measured. Pakistan has three separate land farming divisions (highly acceptable, somewhat sufficient, inappropriate). Pakistan's gross cropland region was projected for 2018-2019 to be 370,200 square kilometers. The statistics of cropland areas produced for Pakistan in this study compared to other sources such as the Pakistan Stats Bureau. But Pakistan, developed from this research, has a high resolution of 10 m to 60 m cropland. Every pixel up to 60-m is approximately 0.099 ha. It allows for the exploitation of areas at the subnational level, often at tiny or broad farm stages. It provides an immense benefit over many cropland goods, as shown in Table 13.

Table 13 Comparisons of farm ground. GEE Satellite Imagery Net Farm Areas focused on data compared with other Pakistan Census Agriculture Organization

Country	Agriculture Suitable Land in Sq. Km (The World Bank Data)	Govt. of Pakistan (Agriculture Census Organization-2010) in Sq. Km.	Net Cropland Area in Sq. Km. (Estimated in Current Study)	Agriculture Land (Pakistan Bureau of Statistics) in Sq. Km.	% of Total Agriculture Land Areas
Pakistan	368,440	274,814	Highly Suitable: 153,900	303,400	47.79%
			Moderate Suitable: 170,300		
			Not Suitable: 46000		
			Total: 370, 200		

4.7 Spatially Distributed Statistical Characteristics of Parameters used in this Study

Spatially Distributed Statistical Characteristics of parameters is presented in following Table 14. Total agriculture land is divided into square kilometre based on the spatially distributed characteristics.

Table 14 Spatially Distributed Statistical Characteristics of Parameters

Slope	The area in Sq. Kilometre	Area%
0-2	77742	21
3-5	99954	27
>5	192504	52
Total Area in Km^2	**370,200**	**100**
Mean Air Temperature Annual	**The area in Sq. Kilometer**	**Area%**
288.15 to 298.15 k	65155.2	17.6
281.15 to 287.15k and 299.15 to 304k	200648.4	54.2
< 281.15 and > 304k	104396.4	28.2
Total Area in Km^2	**370,200**	**100**
Surface Soil Moisture	**The area in Sq. Kilometer**	**Area%**
20-25mm	41832.6	11.3
15-200mm	211384.2	57.1

<15mm	116983.2	31.6
Total Area in Km^2	**370,200**	**100**
Soil pH in H2O	**The area in Sq. Kilometer**	**Area%**
74-78	104396.4	28.2
71-73 and 79-81	145858.8	39.4
<71 and > 81	119944.8	32.4
Total Area in Km^2	**370,200**	**100**

4.8 Discussion

The research shows a 'paradigm changing' by utilizing multi-year satellite imagery data sets from Google Earth Engine to collect high-resolution 10-m to 60 m agriculture land suitability assessment items in very large areas (Pakistan). In the large volume of reference pieces of training and validation datasets from several sources, Naïve Bayes, Random Forest, SVM, CART, and Minimum Distance Machine learning algorithms are used through the Google Earth Engine cloud computing platform for large-scale data management and processing. Similar techniques and strategies have shown that croplands can be measured easily and reliably at wide-scale continental countries with huge dogs numbers. In 2018-19, Pakistan had the highest overall validation accuracy in CART and 95% minimum distance algorithms compared to the other three Machine Learning Algorithms used in this research with the corresponding 60-m agriculture land suitability assessments good.

5 Conclusion and Future Work

5.1 Conclusion

The development and growth of plants and crops heavily depend on the number of mineral nutrients and their concentrations available in the soil, moisture in the soil, air quality and water availability. Plants or crops sometimes face challenges in obtaining a sufficient amount of nutrients for the soil's necessary cellular process due to immobility. The decrease in crops' growth, fertility, or poor food quality happens due to deficiency of natural nutrients, soil moisture, and water, which is required to meet the demand of plants' necessary cellular processes. Lack of nutrients in the soil may result in biodiversity reduction, which directly affects most food webs. This proposed research study will focus on the development of the agriculture land assessment model. Google Earth Engine is a publicly available data repository that hosts an enormous variety of datasets, including climate and weather forecasts, landcover, environmental variables, non-optical and optical wavelengths, water history and classification, and air quality. In this research work, a model will be constructed, predicting land suitability for agriculture activities. The agriculture land evaluation model will be constructed through the analysis of publicly available Google Earth Engine geo-environmental time-series datasets. Machine learning techniques will be applied on Google Earth Engine, geo-environmental imagery datasets for the development of the economic land suitability detection model. Land suitability detection also involves identifying future rainfall situations and situations of future air quality of under consideration land; these factors affect plants' growth. This proposed research study will focus on Pakistan agriculture land, and all training samples will be taken from different cities of Pakistan provinces. Pakistan is one of the largest agricultural countries, and its agriculture sector has a 21% share in GDP, and 72% of Pakistan's land as reported is available for cultivation. The population is rising, and the need is that in combination with others. Over the last ten years, this industry has expanded for food and other goods. As an agricultural basin in Ethiopia, Blue Nile looks like it has similar pleasures. However, the number, the position, and the adequacy point. Don't appear to have been prosecuted. So far, land use in Haphazard has led, particularly on the highland of the basin catchments, to persistent soil erosion, improved and land deterioration. Build development to promote production. By defining opportunities and intrinsic strengths for land objectives. It will help to recognize areas of concern

Control and Potential monitoring approach by technologies for soil or property regeneration. For land suitability testing, methods have been used on blogs around the world for various case studies. This requires a weighted and in-pair study of several methods utilized for land adequacy work for cultivation, biodiversity, and planning on local and national rates. For the evaluation of land suitability, biophysical criteria such as rising, pitch, ground cover and soil properties including group, moisture, cloth and thickness are used. 'Technical judgment' is used for measuring elements to determine the suitability of land Comparison in AHP. The Most standards river drainage in Ethiopia is situated on half of Ethiopia's Part Abbey. It accounts for approximately 20% of the territories of the nation, 50% of its overall annual runoff, 25% of its population and over 40% of its output. The river has a region of 199,812 km2 Divided into 16 catchments, resulting in a wide and rushed highland And Egypt downstream. Biophysical and anthropogenic influences and the runoffs of the highlands' drainage are triggering loss of terrain and soil erosion. The middle/low lands of this basin are a big concern for deforestation. The runoff of field production has been shown to threaten subsistent farmers' livelihoods through land depletion, soil erosion, and development. For geospatial datasets research, the Google Earth engine framework offers numerous machine learning algorithms and a summary of the algorithms given in this report. Information sets accessible from the Google Earth Engine database will be used to address a range of social challenges. In this study paper on the abstract stage, different examples are discussed, demonstrating how we can utilize Google Earth Engine application and data mining to solve social problems. Numerous problems, such as scaling issues, computer process failure and a network application programming interface, are addressed in the final report.

Google Earth Engine provides a parallel high-performance computation service and holds analysis-ready multi-category geospatial datasets in petabytes. Google Earth Engine provides parallel data computation services, visualization of datasets in petabytes volume, and web-based applications prototype development. These services can be controlled and accessed through Google Earth

Engine's own web-based interactive, integrated development environment programming interface (IDE) or GEE supported application programming interface (API). Google Earth Engine data catalogue holds large publicly available geospatial datasets and these datasets are observations of different imaging systems in both non-optical and optical wavelengths and different satellite, land cover, socio-economic, topographic, environmental variables, weather and climate forecast. GEE platform provides data in the preprocessed form and removes the issues associated with data management with the easy-access facility. Further, the user can either access the publicly available geospatial data on Google Earth Engine code editor and can easily analyze the data or can also import private data through the utilization of different GEE API libraries. Google Earth Engine data catalog holds a huge amount of data in petabytes, which are earth observations of satellite and remote sensing imagery of the earth. GEE data catalogue contains Landsat imagery, data of climate forecasts, socio-economic, geophysical, environmental, land cover data, forestry data, snow cover data, and imagery data from Sentinel-1 and Sentinel-2 satellite, and many other kinds of geospatial data. GEE platform provides the facility of uploading private data through REST interface by using the command line or web-based tools, or users can request new additional data in the public data catalogue. Remote sensing earth imagery data in the public catalog is continuously updating at the rate of 6000-scenes per day in case of active missions with a delay of 24 hours after the time of scene acquisitions. Google Earth Engine uses simple and 2D gridded raster bands data model with a lightweight container for images. Google Earth Engine imagery datasets contain a collection of images, and each image metadata consists of various information such as condition under images are collected, time, location, and images metadata associated with key/value. Images in remote sensory imagery data consist of multiple image bands, and each image band can be heterogeneous in projections or data types. However, pixels in bands need to be homogeneous in projections, resolution and data types.

Google Earth Engine provides remote sensing imagery datasets in preprocessed form, which facilitates the user in the process of access and data analysis. GEE combined the related images in the form of the collection because a single sensor sense similar images, usually a collection of related images facilitates users in filtering data or selecting data which meets specific criteria, temporal or specific spatial. For example, in the collection of related images, user can easily extract those images which are captured by satellite in the nighttime with less than 80% cloudy and during any specific day of the year from 2012 to 2016. In Google Earth Engine, images are first to cut into tiles under images' original resolution and projection and then stored into a replicated and efficient tile database. Data ingestion in the form of tiles is a more efficient process than traditional data cube system; this concept of data ingestion usually reduces data degradation and preserve original image resolution, projection, and bit depth.

Google Earth Engine utilizes reduced resolution tiles pyramid concept and reduced resolution tiles are created and stored into tiles databases. This process enabled improved and fast visualization of sensing imagery datasets at the algorithm development stage. The pyramid consists of multiple levels and each level of a pyramid created through down sampling of preceding level by a factor of two, and this process continues until the whole image fit into a single tile. Process of down sampling facilitates during computation and analysis phase when a reduced resolution portion of the image is required at analysis. Only the required tile is retrieved from the appropriate pyramid level. Concept of two factors down sampling helps Google Earth Engine in providing preprocessed data at every scale without introducing storage overhead.

Google Earth Engine public data catalogue holds earth observation data, climate data, environmental data, air quality data, forestry data, socio-economic data and many more other kinds of data, these kinds of data can be utilized in resolving social issues of society or can be utilized in managing of future food need or in planning for preserving air quality for the future generation. Machine Learning or Data mining techniques are playing a major role in the development of intelligent systems intended to use for smart city or social development. Google Earth Engine also provides famous machine learning or data mining algorithms which can be used for the analysis of geospatial datasets, through analysis of geospatial datasets, one can extract inside knowledge from huge data and can utilize in the development of human society. In this study research process, first, a thorough literature review and descriptive study were conducted on Google Erath Engine geo-environmental datasets related to climate, vegetation indexes, elevation, and so on. In the descriptive study of datasets, datasets' features or attributes were identified for analysis purposes at further stages of the research process. At the next stage, a literature review and descriptive study about different machine learning algorithms were conducted for extracting knowledge about the performance and applicability of machine learning algorithms on different data types perspective. The choice of machine learning algorithms and techniques was identified on datasets attributes and descriptive study, which was conducted at an earlier stage. Google Earth Engine provides several climates, water history, and vegetation indexes datasets of more than 20 years long, so the next step of this research study was collecting random training samples after mapping the respective dataset layer on the chosen land boundary. Training samples were taken under both cloudy and not cloudy environments, and collected samples were also belonged from different years. Google Earth Engine also provides cloud-based computation facility for the analysis of petabytes data. Throughout the next step, selected machine-learning algorithms were used to create training data sets, and a land suitability model was developed after a throughout-depth analysis of geo-environmental datasets and machine-learning algorithms. Throughout this report, we looked at the history of the soil, the poisonous gases used in the climate, the drought frequency index of the chosen land (Pakistan Agriculture Land) in order to gain insight into what is going to happen in the short term in relation to the weather and farm nutrition situation. The successful development of plants and crops is attributed to land quality and climate. The research shows a 'paradigm changing' by utilizing multi-year satellite imagery data sets from Google Earth Engine to collect high-resolution 10-m to 60 m agriculture land suitability assessment items in very large areas (Pakistan). In the large volume of reference training and validation datasets from several sources, Naïve Bayes, Random Forest, SVM, CART and Minimum Distance Machine learning algorithms are used through the Google Earth Engine cloud computing platform for large-scale data management and processing. Similar techniques and strategies have shown that croplands can be measured easily and reliably at wide-scale continental countries with huge dogs numbers. In 2018-19, Pakistan had the highest overall validation accuracy in CART and 95% minimum distance algorithms in contrast to other three Machine Learning

Algorithms used in this research with the corresponding 60-m agriculture land suitability assessments goods.

5.2 Future Work

Although land evaluation requires a series of principles, all the criteria' listed are related to the physical environment within this study. The Criteria includes the H_2O surface humidity, pH soil, air temperature, the shape of the soil, soil humidity subsurface, KBDI, pitch, height, and flower field index. These guidelines may raise the evaluation of agricultural output threats. A classification of parameters for the calculation of the suitability index shall be performed throughout this report. Criteria of similar value are clustered together, and the coordinated classes provide equivalent weights to the suitability evaluation. The weightings into the correct matrix, the essential parameters should be viewed individually or as representatives of each class. The definition of prediction action could be used to define the criterion. The research will also be carried out in future work to include plants and various crop varieties and even other plants such as Jatropha, Sporobolus virginity and Distichlis spicate. A detailed study of the capacities and the contribution of desalination plants in remote areas to broad and evapotranspiration environment processes should be performed. However, the study will be extended to determine the effect on suitability maps of the different lands of climate change in the area, which will contribute to a deeper understanding of the impacts of change in climate conditions in the world on food protection and on effective usage of natural resources at the national and local level. To multiple societies, this program should be generalized. When employing more precise methods, sensitivity analysis may be enhanced. Since the findings are compatible with this, the correct fertilizer and its quantity may be shown. In addition, deep learning and ensemble learning methods to boost the performance of the classification process would also be implemented in this framework.

References

ABATZOGLOU, J. T., DOBROWSKI, S. Z., PARKS, S. A. & HEGEWISCH, K. C. 2018. TerraClimate, a high-resolution global dataset of monthly climate and climatic water balance from 1958–2015. *Scientific data,* 5, 170191.

ABDELRAHMAN, M. A., SHALABY, A., ABOELSOUD, M. H. & MOGHANM, F. 2018. GIS spatial model based for determining actual land degradation status in Kafr El-Sheikh Governorate, North Nile Delta. *Modeling Earth Systems and Environment,* 4, 359-372.

AHMED, G. B., SHARIFF, A. R. M., BALASUNDRAM, S. K. & BIN ABDULLAH, A. F. Agriculture land suitability analysis evaluation based multi criteria and GIS approach. IOP Conference Series: Earth and Environmental Science, 2016. 012044.

AHN, C., TORRES, O., LOYOLA, D. G., TIRUCHIRAPALLI, R. & JETHVA, H. T. Aerosol Index Products from Sentinel-5P/TROPOMI and Suomi-NPP/OMPS Measurements. AGU Fall Meeting Abstracts, 2018.

ALDABABSEH, A., TEMIMI, M., MAGHELAL, P., BRANCH, O. & WULFMEYER, V. 2018. Multi-criteria evaluation of irrigated agriculture suitability to achieve food security in an arid environment. *Sustainability,* 10, 803.

ALDABBAS, H., BAJAHZAR, A., ALRUILY, M., QURESHI, A. A., LATIF, R. M. A. & FARHAN, M. 2020. Google Play Content Scraping and Knowledge Engineering using Natural Language Processing Techniques with the Analysis of User Reviews. *Journal of Intelligent Systems,* 30, 192-208.

ALMOTAIRI, M., ALSAHFI, T. & ELMASRI, R. Using Local and Global Divergence Measures to Identify Road Similarity in Different Road Network Datasets. IWCTS@ SIGSPATIAL, 2018. 21-28.

ALONSO, A., MUÑOZ-CARPENA, R., KENNEDY, R. E. & MURCIA, C. 2016. Wetland landscape spatio-temporal degradation dynamics using the new Google Earth Engine cloud-based platform: Opportunities for non-specialists in remote sensing. *Transactions of the ASABE,* 59, 1331-1342.

APPEL, M. & PEBESMA, E. 2019. On-Demand Processing of Data Cubes from Satellite Image Collections with the gdalcubes Library. *Data,* 4, 92.

ASSENG, S., EWERT, F., MARTRE, P., RÖTTER, R. P., LOBELL, D. B., CAMMARANO, D., KIMBALL, B. A., OTTMAN, M. J., WALL, G. & WHITE, J. W. 2015. Rising temperatures reduce global wheat production. *Nature climate change,* 5, 143-147.

AYMEN, A.-T., AL-HUSBAN, Y. & FARHAN, I. 2020. Land suitability evaluation for agricultural use using GIS and remote sensing techniques: The case study of Ma'an Governorate, Jordan. *The Egyptian Journal of Remote Sensing and Space Science.*

BARTKOWIAK, P., CASTELLI, M. & NOTARNICOLA, C. 2019. Downscaling land surface temperature from MODIS dataset with random forest approach over alpine vegetated areas. *Remote Sensing,* 11, 1319.

BASTARRIKA, A., BARRETT, B., ROTETA, E., AKIZU, O., MESANZA, A., TORRE, L., ANAYA, J. A., RODRIGUEZ-MONTELLANO, A. & CHUVIECO, E. 2018. Mapping burned areas in Latin America from 2 Landsat-8 with Google Earth Engine 3.

BEAL COHEN, A. A., SEIFERT, C. A., AZZARI, G. & LOBELL, D. B. 2019. Rotation effects on corn and soybean yield inferred from satellite and field-level data. *Agronomy Journal,* 111, 2940-2948.

BEATON, A., WHALEY, R., CORSTON, K. & KENNY, F. 2019. Identifying historic river ice breakup timing using MODIS and Google Earth Engine in support of operational flood monitoring in Northern Ontario. *Remote sensing of environment,* 224, 352-364.

BERETA, K., CAUMONT, H., DANIELS, U., GOOR, E., KOUBARAKIS, M., PANTAZI, D.-A., STAMOULIS, G., UBELS, S., VENUS, V. & WAHYUDI, F. The Copernicus App Lab project: Easy Access to Copernicus Data. EDBT, 2019. 501-511.

BEVINGTON, A. R., GLEASON, H. E., FOORD, V. N., FLOYD, W. C. & GRIESBAUER, H. P. Regional influence of ocean-climate teleconnections on the timing and duration of MODIS derived snow cover in British Columbia, Canada.

BIKDELI, S. 2019. Redevelopment modeling for land suitability evaluation of the suburb brown-fields using fuzzy logic and GIS, northeastern Iran. *Environment, development and sustainability*, 1-20.

BLANKENAU, P. A. 2017. Bias and Other Error in Gridded Weather Data Sets and Their Impacts on Estimating Reference Evapotranspiration.

BOER, G. J., BAART, F., BRUENS, A., DAMSMA, T., GEER, P., GRASMEIJER, B., HEIJER, K. & KONINGSVELD, M. 2012. OpenEarth: using Google Earth as outreach for NCK's data.

BOSCHETTI, L., ROY, D. P. & JUSTICE, C. 2008. Using NASA's World Wind virtual globe for interactive internet visualization of the global MODIS burned area product. *International Journal of Remote Sensing*, 29, 3067-3072.

BUSKER, T., ROO, A. D., GELATI, E., SCHWATKE, C., ADAMOVIC, M., BISSELINK, B., PEKEL, J.-F. & COTTAM, A. 2019. A global lake and reservoir volume analysis using a surface water dataset and satellite altimetry. *Hydrology and Earth System Sciences,* 23, 669-690.

CARROLL, M. L., TOWNSHEND, J. R., DIMICELI, C. M., NOOJIPADY, P. & SOHLBERG, R. A. 2009. A new global raster water mask at 250 m resolution. *International Journal of Digital Earth*, 2, 291-308.

CHANDOLA, V., VATSAVAI, R. R. & BHADURI, B. iGlobe: an interactive visualization and analysis framework for geospatial data. Proceedings of the 2nd International Conference on Computing for Geospatial Research & Applications, 2011. ACM, 21.

CHAVEZ JR, P. S. 1986. Digital merging of Landsat TM and digitized NHAP data for 1: 24 000-scale image mapping. *Photogrammetric Engineering and Remote Sensing*, 52, 1637-1646.

CHEHADE, W., WEBER, M. & BURROWS, J. 2014. Total ozone trends and variability during 1979–2012 from merged data sets of various satellites. *Atmospheric Chemistry and Physics,* 14, 7059-7074.

CHEN, B., XIAO, X., LI, X., PAN, L., DOUGHTY, R., MA, J., DONG, J., QIN, Y., ZHAO, B. & WU, Z. 2017. A mangrove forest map of China in 2015: Analysis of time series Landsat 7/8 and Sentinel-1A imagery in Google Earth Engine cloud computing platform. *ISPRS Journal of Photogrammetry and Remote Sensing,* 131, 104-120.

CHO, E., JACOBS, J. M., JIA, X. & KRAATZ, S. 2019. Identifying Subsurface Drainage using Satellite Big Data and Machine Learning via Google Earth Engine. *Water Resources Research,* 55, 8028-8045.

CHOI, H. & BINDSCHADLER, R. 2004. Cloud detection in Landsat imagery of ice sheets using shadow matching technique and automatic normalized difference snow index threshold value decision. *Remote Sensing of Environment*, 91, 237-242.

CHRISTENSEN, J., NASH, M., CHALOUD, D. & PITCHFORD, A. 2016. Spatial distributions of small water body types in modified landscapes: lessons from Indiana, USA. *Ecohydrology,* 9, 122-137.

CLARK, M. L. & AIDE, T. M. 2011. Virtual interpretation of Earth Web-Interface Tool (VIEW-IT) for collecting land-use/land-cover reference data. *Remote Sensing,* 3, 601-620.

CONGALTON, R., YADAV, K., MCDONNELL, K., POEHNELT, J., STEVENS, B., GUMMA, M., TELUGUNTLA, P. & THENKABAIL, P. 2017. Global Food Security-support Analysis Data (GFSAD) Cropland Extent 2015 Validation 30 m V001.

DALY, C., SMITH, J. W., SMITH, J. I. & MCKANE, R. B. 2007. High-resolution spatial modeling of daily weather elements for a catchment in the Oregon Cascade Mountains, United States. *Journal of Applied Meteorology and Climatology,* 46, 1565-1586.

DAVIES, D. K., ILAVAJHALA, S., WONG, M. M. & JUSTICE, C. O. 2008. Fire information for resource management system: archiving and distributing MODIS active fire data. *IEEE Transactions on Geoscience and Remote Sensing,* 47, 72-79.

DAVIS, R., YANG, Z., YOST, A., BELONGIE, C. & COHEN, W. 2017. The normal fire environment—Modeling environmental suitability for large forest wildfires using past, present, and future climate normals. *Forest ecology and management,* 390, 173-186.

DEDEOĞLU, M. & DENGIZ, O. 2019. Generating of land suitability index for wheat with hybrid system aproach using AHP and GIS. *Computers and Electronics in Agriculture,* 167, 105062.

DEGUIGNET, M., ARNELL, A., JUFFE-BIGNOLI, D., SHI, Y., BINGHAM, H., MACSHARRY, B. & KINGSTON, N. 2017. Measuring the extent of overlaps in protected area designations. *PloS one,* 12, e0188681.

DENGIZ, O. & USUL, M. 2018. Multi-criteria approach with linear combination technique and analytical hierarchy process in land evaluation studies. *Eurasian Journal of Soil Science,* 7, 20-29.

DONCHYTS, G., SCHELLEKENS, J., WINSEMIUS, H., EISEMANN, E. & VAN DE GIESEN, N. 2016. A 30 m resolution surface water mask including estimation of positional and thematic differences using landsat 8, srtm and openstreetmap: a case study in the Murray-Darling Basin, Australia. *Remote Sensing,* 8, 386.

DONG, J., XIAO, X., MENARGUEZ, M. A., ZHANG, G., QIN, Y., THAU, D., BIRADAR, C. & MOORE III, B. 2016. Mapping paddy rice planting area in northeastern Asia with Landsat 8 images, phenology-based algorithm and Google Earth Engine. *Remote sensing of environment,* 185, 142-154.

EDWARDS, F., ESPOSITO, M. H. & LEE, H. 2018. Risk of police-involved death by race/ethnicity and place, United States, 2012–2018. *American journal of public health,* 108, 1241-1248.

EGAN, P. J. & MULLIN, M. 2016. Recent improvement and projected worsening of weather in the United States. *Nature,* 532, 357.

EL BAROUDY, A. 2016. Mapping and evaluating land suitability using a GIS-based model. *Catena,* 140, 96-104.

ELAALEM, M. 2013. A comparison of parametric and fuzzy multi-criteria methods for evaluating land suitability for olive in Jeffara Plain of Libya. *Apcbee Procedia,* 5, 405-409.

ELHACHAM, E. & ALPERT, P. 2016. Impact of coastline-intensive anthropogenic activities on the atmosphere from moderate resolution imaging spectroradiometer (MODIS) data in Dubai (2001–2014). *Earth's Future,* 4, 54-61.

ELIAS, B. Extracting landmarks with data mining methods. International Conference on Spatial Information Theory, 2003. Springer, 375-389.

ERICKSON, T. A., GUENTCHEV, G. & ROOD, R. B. Generating and Visualizing Climate Indices using Google Earth Engine. AGU Fall Meeting Abstracts, 2017.

ESTRADA, L. L., RASCHE, L. & SCHNEIDER, U. A. 2017. Modeling land suitability for Coffea arabica L. in Central America. *Environmental Modelling & Software,* 95, 196-209.

EYTHORSSON, D., GARDARSSON, S. M., AHMAD, S. K., HOSSAIN, F. & NIJSSEN, B. 2019. Arctic climate and snow cover trends–Comparing Global Circulation Models with remote sensing observations. *International Journal of Applied Earth Observation and Geoinformation,* 80, 71-81.

FEIZIZADEH, B. & BLASCHKE, T. 2013. Land suitability analysis for Tabriz County, Iran: a multi-criteria evaluation approach using GIS. *Journal of Environmental Planning and Management,* 56, 1-23.

FENG, Q., CHAUBEY, I., ENGEL, B., CIBIN, R., SUDHEER, K. & VOLENEC, J. 2017. Marginal land suitability for switchgrass, Miscanthus and hybrid poplar in the Upper Mississippi River Basin (UMRB). *Environmental modelling & software,* 93, 356-365.

FENG, Y., NEGRON-JUAREZ, R. I., PATRICOLA, C. M., COLLINS, W. D., URIARTE, M., HALL, J. S., CLINTON, N. & CHAMBERS, J. Q. 2018. Rapid remote sensing assessment of impacts from Hurricane Maria on forests of Puerto Rico. *PeerJ Preprints,* 6, e26597v1.

FICK, S. E. & HIJMANS, R. J. 2017. WorldClim 2: new 1-km spatial resolution climate surfaces for global land areas. *International journal of climatology,* 37, 4302-4315.

FLOOD, N. 2014. Continuity of reflectance data between Landsat-7 ETM+ and Landsat-8 OLI, for both top-of-atmosphere and surface reflectance: A study in the Australian landscape. *Remote Sensing,* 6, 7952-7970.

FORKUOR, G., HOUNKPATIN, O. K., WELP, G. & THIEL, M. 2017. High resolution mapping of soil properties using remote sensing variables in south-western Burkina Faso: a comparison of machine learning and multiple linear regression models. *PloS one,* 12, e0170478.

FOSTER, M., HEIDINGER, A., HILEY, M., WANZONG, S., WALTHER, A. & BOTAMBEKOV, D. 2016. PATMOS-x Cloud Climate Record Trend Sensitivity to Reanalysis Products. *Remote Sensing,* 8, 424.

FU, X., WANG, X. & YANG, Y. J. 2018. Deriving suitability factors for CA-Markov land use simulation model based on local historical data. *Journal of environmental management,* 206, 10-19.

GAO, F. & ANDERSON, M. Evaluating Yield Variability of Corn and Soybean Using Landsat-8, Sentinel-2 and Modis in Google Earth Engine. IGARSS 2019-2019 IEEE International Geoscience and Remote Sensing Symposium, 2019. IEEE, 7286-7289.

GAO, F., ANDERSON, M. C., KUSTAS, W. P. & WANG, Y. 2012. Simple method for retrieving leaf area index from Landsat using MODIS leaf area index products as reference. *Journal of Applied Remote Sensing,* 6, 063554.

GASPARINI, K. A. C., SILVA JUNIOR, C. H. L., SHIMABUKURO, Y. E., ARAI, E., SILVA, C. A. & MARSHALL, P. L. 2019. Determining a Threshold to Delimit the Amazonian Forests from the Tree Canopy Cover 2000 GFC Data. *Sensors,* 19, 5020.

GIRI, C., PENGRA, B., LONG, J. & LOVELAND, T. R. 2013. Next generation of global land cover characterization, mapping, and monitoring. *International Journal of Applied Earth Observation and Geoinformation,* 25, 30-37.

GOETZ, S. J., BACCINI, A., LAPORTE, N. T., JOHNS, T., WALKER, W., KELLNDORFER, J., HOUGHTON, R. A. & SUN, M. 2009. Mapping and monitoring carbon stocks with satellite observations: a comparison of methods. *Carbon balance and management,* 4, 2.

GOLDBLATT, R., YOU, W., HANSON, G. & KHANDELWAL, A. 2016. Detecting the boundaries of urban areas in india: A dataset for pixel-based image classification in google earth engine. *Remote Sensing,* 8, 634.

GORDON, L. J., STEFFEN, W., JÖNSSON, B. F., FOLKE, C., FALKENMARK, M. & JOHANNESSEN, Å. 2005. Human modification of global water vapor flows from the land surface. *Proceedings of the National Academy of Sciences,* 102, 7612-7617.

GORELICK, N., HANCHER, M., DIXON, M., ILYUSHCHENKO, S., THAU, D. & MOORE, R. 2017. Google Earth Engine: Planetary-scale geospatial analysis for everyone. *Remote sensing of Environment,* 202, 18-27.

GRIFFIN, D., SIORIS, C., CHEN, J., DICKSON, N. & KOVACHIK, A. The 2018 fire season in North America as seen by TROPOMI: aerosol layer height validation and evaluation of model-derived plume heights.

GUTMAN, G., HUANG, C., CHANDER, G., NOOJIPADY, P. & MASEK, J. G. 2013. Assessment of the NASA–USGS global land survey (GLS) datasets. *Remote sensing of environment,* 134, 249-265.

HADIPOUR, A., VAFAIE, F. & HADIPOUR, V. 2015. Land suitability evaluation for brackish water aquaculture development in coastal area of Hormozgan, Iran. *Aquaculture international,* 23, 329-343.

HAGENAARS, G., LUIJENDIJK, A., DE VRIES, S., DE BOER, W., HAGENAARS, G., LUIJENDIJK, A., DE VRIES, S. & DE BOER, W. 2017. Long term coastline monitoring derived from satellite imagery. *Coastal Dynamics 2017.*

HAKDAOUI, S., EMRAN, A., PRADHAN, B., ABDELJEBBAR, Q., BALLA, T. E., MFONDOUM, A. H. N., LEE, C.-W. & ALAMRI, A. M. 2020. Assessing the Changes in the Moisture/Dryness of Water Cavity Surfaces in Imlili Sebkha in Southwestern Morocco by Using Machine Learning Classification in Google Earth Engine. *Remote Sensing,* 12, 131.

HAMZEH, S., MOKARRAM, M., HARATIAN, A., BARTHOLOMEUS, H., LIGTENBERG, A. & BREGT, A. K. 2016. Feature selection as a time and cost-saving approach for land suitability classification (case study of Shavur Plain, Iran). *Agriculture,* 6, 52.

HANSEN, M. C., POTAPOV, P. V., MOORE, R., HANCHER, M., TURUBANOVA, S. A., TYUKAVINA, A., THAU, D., STEHMAN, S., GOETZ, S. J. & LOVELAND, T. R. 2013. High-resolution global maps of 21st-century forest cover change. *science,* 342, 850-853.

HATFIELD, J. L. & PRUEGER, J. H. 2015. Temperature extremes: Effect on plant growth and development. *Weather and climate extremes,* 10, 4-10.

HE, M., KIMBALL, J. S., MANETA, M. P., MAXWELL, B. D., MORENO, A., BEGUERÍA, S. & WU, X. 2018. Regional crop gross primary productivity and yield estimation using fused landsat-MODIS data. *Remote Sensing,* 10, 372.

HENSHAW, A. J., SEKARSARI, P. W., ZOLEZZI, G. & GURNELL, A. M. 2019. Google Earth as a data source for investigating river forms and processes: Discriminating river types using form-based process indicators. *Earth Surface Processes and Landforms.*

HÖRSCH, J., HOFMANN, F., SCHLACHTBERGER, D. & BROWN, T. 2018. PyPSA-Eur: An open optimisation model of the European transmission system. *Energy strategy reviews,* 22, 207-215.

HU, Y. & HU, Y. 2019. Land Cover Changes and Their Driving Mechanisms in Central Asia from 2001 to 2017 Supported by Google Earth Engine. *Remote Sensing,* 11, 554.

HUANG, H., CHEN, Y., CLINTON, N., WANG, J., WANG, X., LIU, C., GONG, P., YANG, J., BAI, Y. & ZHENG, Y. 2017. Mapping major land cover dynamics in Beijing using all Landsat images in Google Earth Engine. *Remote Sensing of Environment,* 202, 166-176.

HUBERT, D., KEPPEN, A., VERHOELST, T., GRANVILLE, J., LAMBERT, J.-C., HEUE, K.-P., PEDERGNANA, M., LOYOLA, D., EICHMANN, K.-U. & WEBER, M. 2019. Ground-based Assessment of the First Year of Sentinel-5p Tropospheric Ozone Data.

HULLEY, G. C., HOOK, S. J., ABBOTT, E., MALAKAR, N., ISLAM, T. & ABRAMS, M. 2015. The ASTER Global Emissivity Dataset (ASTER GED): Mapping Earth's emissivity at 100 meter spatial scale. *Geophysical Research Letters,* 42, 7966-7976.

HUNTINGTON, J. L., HEGEWISCH, K. C., DAUDERT, B., MORTON, C. G., ABATZOGLOU, J. T., MCEVOY, D. J. & ERICKSON, T. 2017. Climate Engine: cloud computing and visualization of climate and remote sensing data for advanced natural resource monitoring and process understanding. *Bulletin of the American Meteorological Society,* 98, 2397-2410.

IRZAK, O., THOMAS, A., SCHNEIDER, S. & VOSS, C. Predicting Arctic Methane Seeps via Satellite Imagery.

JAMEI, Y., RAJAGOPALAN, P. & SUN, Q. C. 2019. Time-series dataset on land surface temperature, vegetation, built up areas and other climatic factors in top 20 global cities (2000–2018). *Data in brief,* 23.

JAY, S., POTTER, C., CRABTREE, R., GENOVESE, V., WEISS, D. J. & KRAFT, M. 2016. Evaluation of modelled net primary production using MODIS and landsat satellite data fusion. *Carbon balance and management,* 11, 8.

JIN, G., WANG, Z., HU, X., HU, S. & ZHANG, D. 2013. Land suitability evaluation in the Qinghai-Tibet Plateau based on fuzzy weight of evidence model. *Transactions of the Chinese Society of Agricultural Engineering,* 29, 241-250.

JOHANSEN, K., PHINN, S. & TAYLOR, M. 2015. Mapping woody vegetation clearing in Queensland, Australia from Landsat imagery using the Google Earth Engine. *Remote Sensing Applications: Society and Environment,* 1, 36-49.

JOSHI, A. R., DINERSTEIN, E., WIKRAMANAYAKE, E., ANDERSON, M. L., OLSON, D., JONES, B. S., SEIDENSTICKER, J., LUMPKIN, S., HANSEN, M. C. & SIZER, N. C. 2016. Tracking changes and preventing loss in critical tiger habitat. *Science advances,* 2, e1501675.

JURKOWSKI, C., BAQAI, A., OCHOA, J. I., WILLIAMS, A., WEBER, K. T., TREC, G., LAUER, I., MACEK, C., ZUREK, F. & BRODDLE, M. 2019. Evaluating Evapotranspiration in Humid

Subtropical and Semi-Arid Climates with NASA Earth Observations to Understand Water Balance in Paraná and the Patagonia Steppe of Argentina.

KALOGIROU, S. 2002. Expert systems and GIS: an application of land suitability evaluation. *Computers, environment and urban systems,* 26, 89-112.

KARIMI, F., SULTANA, S., SHIRZADI BABAKAN, A. & ROYALL, D. 2018. Land suitability evaluation for organic agriculture of wheat using GIS and multicriteria analysis. *Papers in Applied Geography,* 4, 326-342.

KAZEMI, H. & AKINCI, H. 2018. A land use suitability model for rainfed farming by Multi-criteria Decision-making Analysis (MCDA) and Geographic Information System (GIS). *Ecological Engineering,* 116, 1-6.

KELLEY, L., PITCHER, L. & BACON, C. 2018. Using Google Earth Engine to Map Complex Shade-Grown Coffee Landscapes in Northern Nicaragua. *Remote Sensing,* 10, 952.

KHAN, N. A., BROHI, S. N. & JHANJHI, N. 2020a. UAV's Applications, Architecture, Security Issues and Attack Scenarios: A Survey. *Intelligent Computing and Innovation on Data Science.* Springer.

KHAN, R., GILANI, H., IQBAL, N. & SHAHID, I. 2020b. Satellite-based (2000–2015) drought hazard assessment with indices, mapping, and monitoring of Potohar plateau, Punjab, Pakistan. *Environmental Earth Sciences,* 79, 23.

KHORRAM, S., BROCKHAUS, J. A. & CHESHIRE, H. M. 1987. Comparson of landsat mss and tm data for urban land-use classification. *IEEE transactions on geoscience and remote sensing,* 238-243.

KIM, Y.-A. 2018. Examining the relationship between the structural characteristics of place and crime by imputing census block data in street segments: Is the pain worth the gain? *Journal of Quantitative Criminology,* 34, 67-110.

KORSUNSKA, Y., SHUMILO, L., KOLOTII, A. & SHELESTOV, A. Air Quality Estimation Using Satellite and In-situ Data for Kyiv City within ERA-PLANET Project. 2019 IEEE 2nd Ukraine Conference on Electrical and Computer Engineering (UKRCON), 2019. IEEE, 1032-1036.

KOTSIANTIS, S. B. 2013. Decision trees: a recent overview. *Artificial Intelligence Review,* 39, 261-283.

KOULGI, P. S., CLINTON, N. & KARANTH, K. K. 2019. Extensive vegetation browning and drying in forests of India's Tiger Reserves. *Scientific reports,* 9, 1-12.

LAL, R. 2016. Soil Health and Carbon Management. Food and Energy Security, 5, 212-222.

LATIF, R. M. A., ABDULLAH, M. T., SHAH, S. U. A., FARHAN, M., IJAZ, F. & KARIM, A. Data Scraping from Google Play Store and Visualization of its Content for Analytics. 2019 2nd International Conference on Computing, Mathematics and Engineering Technologies (iCoMET), 2019a. IEEE, 1-8.

LATIF, R. M. A., BELHAOUARI, S. B., SAEED, S., IMRAN, L. B., SADIQ, M. & FARHAN, M. 2020. Integration of Google Play Content and Frost Prediction Using CNN: Scalable IoT Framework for Big Data. *IEEE Access,* 8, 6890-6900.

LATIF, R. M. A., UMER, M., TARIQ, T., FARHAN, M., RIZWAN, O. & ALI, G. A Smart Methodology for Analyzing Secure E-Banking and E-Commerce Websites. 2019 16th International Bhurban Conference on Applied Sciences and Technology (IBCAST), 2019b. IEEE, 589-596.

LAUER, I., JURKOWSKI, C., MACEK, C., ZUREK, F., WEBER, K. T., TREC, G., BRODDLE, M., COATS, D., KUCERA, L. & SFORZO, Z. 2018. Evaluating Evapotranspiration and Water Budget Components in Semi-Arid Sagebrush Steppe.

LAWSON, C. T. 2018. Applying Census Data for Transportation: 50 Years of Transportation Planning Data Progress. *Transportation Research Circular.*

LEE, J. S. H., WICH, S., WIDAYATI, A. & KOH, L. P. 2016. Detecting industrial oil palm plantations on Landsat images with Google Earth Engine. *Remote Sensing Applications: Society and Environment,* 4, 219-224.

LENSKY, I. M., DAYAN, U. & HELMAN, D. 2018. Synoptic Circulation Impact on the Near-Surface Temperature Difference Outweighs That of the Seasonal Signal in the Eastern Mediterranean. *Journal of Geophysical Research: Atmospheres,* 123, 11,333-11,347.

LI, G., MESSINA, J. P., PETER, B. G. & SNAPP, S. S. 2017. Mapping land suitability for agriculture in Malawi. *Land degradation & development,* 28, 2001-2016.

LI, L., YANG, J. & WU, J. 2019. A Method of Watershed Delineation for Flat Terrain Using Sentinel-2A Imagery and DEM: A Case Study of the Taihu Basin. *ISPRS International Journal of Geo-Information,* 8, 528.

LI, Z., LIU, C., ZHANG, P. & TIAN, B. Assessment of Snow Cover Product Using Google Earth Engine Cloud Computing Platform. IGARSS 2018-2018 IEEE International Geoscience and Remote Sensing Symposium, 2018. IEEE, 5203-5205.

LIM, M., ABDULLAH, A. & JHANJHI, N. 2020. Data Fusion-Link Prediction for Evolutionary Network with Deep Reinforcement Learning. *methodology,* 11.

LIOU, Y.-A. & MULUALEM, G. M. 2019. Spatio–temporal Assessment of Drought in Ethiopia and the Impact of Recent Intense Droughts. *Remote Sensing,* 11, 1828.

LIU, X., HU, G., CHEN, Y., LI, X., XU, X., LI, S., PEI, F. & WANG, S. 2018. High-resolution multi-temporal mapping of global urban land using Landsat images based on the Google Earth Engine Platform. *Remote sensing of environment,* 209, 227-239.

LONG, T., ZHANG, Z., HE, G., JIAO, W., TANG, C., WU, B., ZHANG, X., WANG, G. & YIN, R. 2019. 30 m Resolution Global Annual Burned Area Mapping Based on Landsat Images and Google Earth Engine. *Remote Sensing,* 11, 489.

LÜTJENS, M., KERSTEN, T. P., DORSCHEL, B. & TSCHIRSCHWITZ, F. 2019. Virtual Reality in Cartography: Immersive 3D Visualization of the Arctic Clyde Inlet (Canada) Using Digital Elevation Models and Bathymetric Data. *Multimodal Technologies and Interaction,* 3, 9.

LYONS, E. A. & SHENG, Y. 2018. Laketime: Automated seasonal scene selection for global lake mapping using landsat etm+ and oli. *Remote Sensing,* 10, 54.

MAHDIANPARI, M., SALEHI, B., MOHAMMADIMANESH, F., HOMAYOUNI, S. & GILL, E. 2019. The first wetland inventory map of newfoundland at a spatial resolution of 10 m using sentinel-1 and sentinel-2 data on the google earth engine cloud computing platform. *Remote Sensing,* 11, 43.

MALEKI, F., KAZEMI, H., SIAHMARGUEE, A. & KAMKAR, B. 2017. Development of a land use suitability model for saffron (Crocus sativus L.) cultivation by multi-criteria evaluation and spatial analysis. *Ecological Engineering,* 106, 140-153.

MANDAL, D., KUMAR, V., BHATTACHARYA, A., RAO, Y. S., SIQUEIRA, P. & BERA, S. 2018. Sen4Rice: A processing chain for differentiating early and late transplanted rice using time-series Sentinel-1 SAR data with Google Earth engine. *IEEE Geoscience and Remote Sensing Letters,* 15, 1947-1951.

MANI, A. & TSAI, F. T.-C. 2016. Ensemble averaging methods for quantifying uncertainty sources in modeling climate change impact on runoff projection. *Journal of Hydrologic Engineering,* 22, 04016067.

MAO, F., PAN, Z., HENDERSON, D. S., WANG, W. & GONG, W. 2018. Vertically resolved physical and radiative response of ice clouds to aerosols during the Indian summer monsoon season. *Remote Sensing of Environment,* 216, 171-182.

MBUGUA, J. K. & SUKSA-NGIAM, W. 2018. Predicting Suitable Areas for Growing Cassava Using Remote Sensing and Machine Learning Techniques: A Study in Nakhon-Phanom Thailand. *Issues in Informing Science and Information Technology,* 15, 043-056.

MEDINA-LOPEZ, E. & UREÑA-FUENTES, L. 2019. High-Resolution Sea Surface Temperature and Salinity in Coastal Areas Worldwide from Raw Satellite Data. *Remote Sensing,* 11, 2191.

MEMARBASHI, E., AZADI, H., BARATI, A. A., MOHAJERI, F., PASSEL, S. V. & WITLOX, F. 2017. Land-use suitability in Northeast Iran: application of AHP-GIS hybrid model. *ISPRS International Journal of Geo-Information,* 6, 396.

MESGARAN, M. B., MADANI, K., HASHEMI, H. & AZADI, P. 2017. Iran's land suitability for agriculture. *Scientific reports,* 7, 1-12.

MIDEKISA, A., HOLL, F., SAVORY, D. J., ANDRADE-PACHECO, R., GETHING, P. W., BENNETT, A. & STURROCK, H. J. 2017. Mapping land cover change over continental Africa using Landsat and Google Earth Engine cloud computing. *PloS one,* 12, e0184926.

MITRAKA, Z., BENAS, N., GORELICK, N. & CHRYSOULAKIS, N. Global land surface albedo maps from MODIS using the Google Earth Engine. EGU General Assembly Conference Abstracts, 2016.

MOHITE, J., SAWANT, S., RANA, S. & PAPPULA, S. 2019. WHEAT AREA MAPPING AND PHENOLOGY DETECTION USING SYNTHETIC APERTURE RADAR AND MULTI MULTI-SPECTRAL REMOTE SENSING OBSERVATIONS. *International Archives of the Photogrammetry, Remote Sensing & Spatial Information Sciences.*

MOKARRAM, M., HAMZEH, S., AMINZADEH, F. & ZAREI, A. R. 2015. Using machine learning for land suitability classification. *West African Journal of Applied Ecology,* 23, 63-73.

MONDAL, P., TRZASKA, S. & DE SHERBININ, A. 2018. Landsat-derived estimates of mangrove extents in the sierra leone coastal landscape complex during 1990–2016. *Sensors,* 18, 12.

MONTGOMERY, B., DRAGIĆEVIĆ, S., DUJMOVIĆ, J. & SCHMIDT, M. 2016. A GIS-based Logic Scoring of Preference method for evaluation of land capability and suitability for agriculture. *Computers and Electronics in Agriculture,* 124, 340-353.

MOSLEH, Z., SALEHI, M. H., FASAKHODI, A. A., JAFARI, A., MEHNATKESH, A. & BORUJENI, I. E. 2017. Sustainable allocation of agricultural lands and water resources using suitability analysis and mathematical multi-objective programming. *Geoderma,* 303, 52-59.

MUCHE, M. E., SINNATHAMBY, S., PARMAR, R., KNIGHTES, C. D., JOHNSTON, J. M., WOLFE, K., PURUCKER, S. T., CYTERSKI, M. J. & SMITH, D. 2019. Comparison and Evaluation of Gridded Precipitation Datasets in a Kansas Agricultural Watershed Using SWAT. *JAWRA Journal of the American Water Resources Association.*

MÜLLER, R. D., QIN, X., SANDWELL, D. T., DUTKIEWICZ, A., WILLIAMS, S. E., FLAMENT, N., MAUS, S. & SETON, M. 2016. The GPlates portal: cloud-based interactive 3D visualization of global geophysical and geological data in a web browser. *PloS one,* 11, e0150883.

MUNDIA, C. N. 2015. Land suitability assessment for effective crop production, a case study of Taita Hills, Kenya.

MURTHY, K., SHEARN, M., SMILEY, B. D., CHAU, A. H., LEVINE, J. & ROBINSON, M. D. SkySat-1: very high-resolution imagery from a small satellite. Sensors, Systems, and Next-Generation Satellites XVIII, 2014. International Society for Optics and Photonics, 92411E.

NASCETTI, A., DI RITA, M., RAVANELLI, R., AMICUZI, M., ESPOSITO, S. & CRESPI, M. 2017. FREE GLOBAL DSM ASSESSMENT ON LARGE SCALE AREAS EXPLOITING THE POTENTIALITIES OF THE INNOVATIVE GOOGLE EARTH ENGINE PLATFORM. *International Archives of the Photogrammetry, Remote Sensing & Spatial Information Sciences,* 42.

NGUYEN, T. T., VERDOODT, A., VAN Y, T., DELBECQUE, N., TRAN, T. C. & VAN RANST, E. 2015. Design of a GIS and multi-criteria based land evaluation procedure for sustainable land-use planning at the regional level. *Agriculture, Ecosystems & Environment,* 200, 1-11.

NIKRAFTAR, Z., RAJABI-KIASARI, S. & SEYDI, S. 2019. GENETIC ALGORITHM BASED FEATURE SELECTION FOR LANDSLIDE SUSCEPTIBILITY MAPPING IN NORTHERN IRAN. *International Archives of the Photogrammetry, Remote Sensing & Spatial Information Sciences.*

NIVEDITA PRIYADARSHINI, K., SIVASHANKARI, V. & SHEKHAR, S. 2019. AN ASSESSMENT OF LAND COVER CHANGE DYNAMICS OF GAJA CYCLONE IN COASTAL TAMIL NADU, INDIA USING SENTINEL 1 SAR DATASET. *International Archives of the Photogrammetry, Remote Sensing & Spatial Information Sciences.*

OKSANEN, J. 2006. Digital elevation model error in terrain analysis.

OMERNIK, J. M., GRIFFITH, G. E., HUGHES, R. M., GLOVER, J. B. & WEBER, M. H. 2017. How misapplication of the hydrologic unit framework diminishes the meaning of watersheds. *Environmental management,* 60, 1-11.

OMRANI, H., OMRANI, B., PARMENTIER, B. & HELBICH, M. 2020. Spatio-temporal data on the air pollutant nitrogen dioxide derived from Sentinel satellite for France. *Data in Brief,* 105089.

OSTOVARI, Y., HONARBAKHSH, A., SANGOONY, H., ZOLFAGHARI, F., MALEKI, K. & INGRAM, B. 2019. GIS and multi-criteria decision-making analysis assessment of land suitability for rapeseed farming in calcareous soils of semi-arid regions. *Ecological indicators,* 103, 479-487.

OTGONBAYAR, M., ATZBERGER, C., CHAMBERS, J., AMARSAIKHAN, D., BÖCK, S. & TSOGTBAYAR, J. 2017. Land suitability evaluation for agricultural cropland in Mongolia using the spatial MCDM method and AHP based GIS. *Journal of Geoscience and Environment Protection,* 5, 238-263.

PADARIAN, J., MINASNY, B. & MCBRATNEY, A. B. 2015. Using Google's cloud-based platform for digital soil mapping. *Computers & Geosciences,* 83, 80-88.

PARASTATIDIS, D., MITRAKA, Z., CHRYSOULAKIS, N. & ABRAMS, M. 2017. Online global land surface temperature estimation from landsat. *Remote Sensing,* 9, 1208.

PATEL, N. N., ANGIULI, E., GAMBA, P., GAUGHAN, A., LISINI, G., STEVENS, F. R., TATEM, A. J. & TRIANNI, G. 2015. Multitemporal settlement and population mapping from Landsat using Google Earth Engine. *International Journal of Applied Earth Observation and Geoinformation,* 35, 199-208.

PEREIRA, J. M. 2003. Remote sensing of burned areas in tropical savannas. *International Journal of Wildland Fire,* 12, 259-270.

PILEVAR, A. R., MATINFAR, H. R., SOHRABI, A. & SARMADIAN, F. 2020. Integrated fuzzy, AHP and GIS techniques for land suitability assessment in semi-arid regions for wheat and maize farming. *Ecological Indicators,* 110, 105887.

PINHEIRO, D., HARTMAN, R., ROMERO, E., MENEZES, R. & CADEIRAS, M. 2019. Network-Based Delineation of Health Service Areas: A Comparative Analysis of Community Detection Algorithms. *arXiv preprint arXiv:1912.08921.*

POLIYAPRAM, V., IMAMOGLU, N. & NAKAMURA, R. Deep Learning Model for Water/Ice/Land Classification Using Large-Scale Medium Resolution Satellite Images. IGARSS 2019-2019 IEEE International Geoscience and Remote Sensing Symposium, 2019. IEEE, 3884-3887.

POTTER, N., BRADY, M. P. & RAJAGOPALAN, K. 2018. Using Climate Analogues to Obtain a Causal Estimate of the Impact of Climate on Agricultural Productivity.

POTTIER, C., GARÇON, V., LARNICOL, G., SUDRE, J., SCHAEFFER, P. & LE TRAON, P.-Y. 2006. Merging SeaWiFS and MODIS/Aqua ocean color data in North and Equatorial Atlantic using weighted averaging and objective analysis. *IEEE transactions on geoscience and remote sensing,* 44, 3436-3451.

POURGHASEMI, H. R., JIRANDEH, A. G., PRADHAN, B., XU, C. & GOKCEOGLU, C. 2013. Landslide susceptibility mapping using support vector machine and GIS at the Golestan Province, Iran. *Journal of Earth System Science,* 122, 349-369.

PRAMANIK, M. K. 2016. Site suitability analysis for agricultural land use of Darjeeling district using AHP and GIS techniques. *Modeling Earth Systems and Environment,* 2, 56.

PRIVETTE, J. L., BATES, J., KARL, T., BARKSTROM, B., KEARNS, E. & MARKHAM, D. J13. 2 NOAA'S APPROACH TO PROVIDING CLIMATE DATA RECORDS (CDRs) IN COORDINATION WITH OTHER US AGENCY ACTIVITIES.

QIN, Y., XIAO, X., WANG, J., DONG, J., EWING, K., HOAGLAND, B., HOUGH, D., FAGIN, T., ZOU, Z. & GEISSLER, G. 2016. Mapping annual forest cover in sub-humid and semi-arid regions through analysis of Landsat and PALSAR imagery. *Remote Sensing,* 8, 933.

QIU, F., CHASTAIN, B., ZHOU, Y., ZHANG, C. & SRIDHARAN, H. 2014. Modeling land suitability/capability using fuzzy evaluation. *GeoJournal,* 79, 167-182.

RAHIM, S. E., SUPLI, A. A., DAMIRI, N., ZAMAN, C. & HUSIN, H. 2019. Evaluation tool of land suitability for medicinal plants. *Sriwijaya Journal of Environment,* 4, 1-6.

RAMZAN, M., AWAN, S. M., ALDABBAS, H., ABID, A., FARHAN, M., KHALID, S. & LATIF, R. M. A. 2019. Internet of medical things for smart D3S to enable road safety. *International Journal of Distributed Sensor Networks,* 15, 1550147719864883.

RAUP, B., RACOVITEANU, A., KHALSA, S. J. S., HELM, C., ARMSTRONG, R. & ARNAUD, Y. 2007. The GLIMS geospatial glacier database: a new tool for studying glacier change. *Global and Planetary Change,* 56, 101-110.

REHMAN, A., JINGDONG, L., SHAHZAD, B., CHANDIO, A. A., HUSSAIN, I., NABI, G. & IQBAL, M. S. 2015. Economic perspectives of major field crops of Pakistan: An empirical study. *Pacific science review b: humanities and social sciences,* 1, 145-158.

RESHMIDEVI, T., ELDHO, T. & JANA, R. 2009. A GIS-integrated fuzzy rule-based inference system for land suitability evaluation in agricultural watersheds. *Agricultural systems,* 101, 101-109.

RUTKOWSKI, J., CANTY, M. J. & NIELSEN, A. A. 2018. Site monitoring with sentinel-1 dual polarization sar imagery using google earth engine. *Journal of Nuclear Materials Management,* 46, 48-59.

SAEED, S., ABDULLAH, A. & JHANJHI, N. 2019. Analysis of the lung cancer patient's for data mining tool. *IJCSNS,* 19, 90.

SAEED, S., JHANJHI, N., NAQVI, M., PONNUSAMY, V. & HUMAYUN, M. 2020. Analysis of Climate Prediction and Climate Change in Pakistan Using Data Mining Techniques. *Industrial Internet of Things and Cyber-Physical Systems: Transforming the Conventional to Digital.* IGI Global.

SAKIEH, Y., SALMANMAHINY, A., JAFARNEZHAD, J., MEHRI, A., KAMYAB, H. & GALDAVI, S. 2015. Evaluating the strategy of decentralized urban land-use planning in a developing region. *Land use policy,* 48, 534-551.

SANTILLAN, J. R., MAKINANO-SANTILLAN, M. & MAKINANO, R. M. Vertical accuracy assessment of ALOS World 3D-30M Digital Elevation Model over northeastern Mindanao, Philippines. 2016 IEEE International Geoscience and Remote Sensing Symposium (IGARSS), 2016. IEEE, 5374-5377.

SAZIB, N., MLADENOVA, I. & BOLTEN, J. 2018. Leveraging the google earth engine for drought assessment using global soil moisture data. *Remote Sensing,* 10, 1265.

SEYEDMOHAMMADI, J., SARMADIAN, F., JAFARZADEH, A. A. & MCDOWELL, R. W. 2019. Development of a model using matter element, AHP and GIS techniques to assess the suitability of land for agriculture. *Geoderma,* 352, 80-95.

SHELESTOV, A., LAVRENIUK, M., KUSSUL, N., NOVIKOV, A. & SKAKUN, S. Large scale crop classification using Google earth engine platform. 2017 IEEE International Geoscience and Remote Sensing Symposium (IGARSS), 2017. IEEE, 3696-3699.

SHI, T., ZHENG, G., WANG, Z. & WANG, L. 2007. Progress in research on land suitability evaluation in China. *Progress in Geography,* 26, 106-115.

SIDHU, N., PEBESMA, E. & CÂMARA, G. 2018. Using Google Earth Engine to detect land cover change: Singapore as a use case. *European Journal of Remote Sensing,* 51, 486-500.

SWARTZ, W., SALA, E., TRACEY, S., WATSON, R. & PAULY, D. 2010. The spatial expansion and ecological footprint of fisheries (1950 to present). *PloS one,* 5, e15143.

TAGHIZADEH-MEHRJARDI, R., NABIOLLAHI, K., RASOLI, L., KERRY, R. & SCHOLTEN, T. 2020. Land Suitability Assessment and Agricultural Production Sustainability Using Machine Learning Models. *Agronomy,* 10, 573.

TALLAT, R., LATIF, R. M. A., ALI, G., ZAHEER, A. N., FARHAN, M. & SHAH, S. U. A. Visualization and Analytics of Biological Data by Using Different Tools and Techniques.

2019 16th International Bhurban Conference on Applied Sciences and Technology (IBCAST), 2019. IEEE, 291-303.

TANG, Z., LI, Y., GU, Y., JIANG, W., XUE, Y., HU, Q., LAGRANGE, T., BISHOP, A., DRAHOTA, J. & LI, R. 2016. Assessing Nebraska playa wetland inundation status during 1985–2015 using Landsat data and Google Earth Engine. *Environmental monitoring and assessment,* 188, 654.

TARIQ, T., LATIF, R. M. A., FARHAN, M., ABBAS, A. & IJAZ, F. A smart heart beat analytics system using wearable device. 2019 2nd International Conference on Communication, Computing and Digital systems (C-CODE), 2019. IEEE, 137-142.

TELUGUNTLA, P., THENKABAIL, P. S., OLIPHANT, A., XIONG, J., GUMMA, M. K., CONGALTON, R. G., YADAV, K. & HUETE, A. 2018. A 30-m landsat-derived cropland extent product of Australia and China using random forest machine learning algorithm on Google Earth Engine cloud computing platform. *ISPRS Journal of Photogrammetry and Remote Sensing,* 144, 325-340.

THEYS, N., SMEDT, I. D., YU, H., DANCKAERT, T., GENT, J. V., HÖRMANN, C., WAGNER, T., HEDELT, P., BAUER, H. & ROMAHN, F. 2017. Sulfur dioxide retrievals from TROPOMI onboard Sentinel-5 Precursor: algorithm theoretical basis. *Atmospheric Measurement Techniques,* 10.

TUNG, N. T. & SON, T. P. H. GIS-Based Multi-Criteria Evaluation Models for Selection of Suitable Sites for Pacific Oyster (Crassostrea gigas) Aquaculture in the Central Region of Vietnam.

USHIO, T. & KACHI, M. 2010. Kalman filtering applications for global satellite mapping of precipitation (GSMaP). *Satellite rainfall applications for surface hydrology.* Springer.

UZHINSKIY, A., OSOSKOV, G., GONCHAROV, P. & FRONTSYEVA, M. 2018. Combining satellite imagery and machine learning to predict atmospheric heavy metal contamination. *Advisory committee,* 145.

VALADE, S., LEY, A., MASSIMETTI, F., D'HONDT, O., LAIOLO, M., COPPOLA, D., LOIBL, D., HELLWICH, O. & WALTER, T. R. 2019. Towards Global Volcano Monitoring Using Multisensor Sentinel Missions and Artificial Intelligence: The MOUNTS Monitoring System. *Remote Sensing,* 11, 1528.

VAZ, A. S., GONÇALVES, J. F., PEREIRA, P., SANTARÉM, F., VICENTE, J. R. & HONRADO, J. P. 2019. Earth observation and social media: Evaluating the spatiotemporal contribution of non-native trees to cultural ecosystem services. *Remote Sensing of Environment,* 230, 111193.

VINCENT, D. R., DEEPA, N., ELAVARASAN, D., SRINIVASAN, K., CHAUHDARY, S. H. & IWENDI, C. 2019. Sensors driven AI-based agriculture recommendation model for assessing land suitability. *Sensors,* 19, 3667.

VOSE, R. S., ARNDT, D., BANZON, V. F., EASTERLING, D. R., GLEASON, B., HUANG, B., KEARNS, E., LAWRIMORE, J. H., MENNE, M. J. & PETERSON, T. C. 2012. NOAA's merged land–ocean surface temperature analysis. *Bulletin of the American Meteorological Society,* 93, 1677-1685.

WALI, E., DATTA, A., SHRESTHA, R. P. & SHRESTHA, S. 2016. Development of a land suitability model for saffron (Crocus sativus L.) cultivation in Khost Province of Afghanistan using GIS and AHP techniques. *Archives of Agronomy and Soil science,* 62, 921-934.

WANG, D., SHEN, R., HUANG, X. & SHI, C. An integrated GIS application system for soil moisture data assimilation. International Symposium on Optoelectronic Technology and Application 2014: Optical Remote Sensing Technology and Applications, 2014. International Society for Optics and Photonics, 92990J.

WANG, J., ZHAO, F., YANG, J. & LI, X. 2017. Mining site reclamation planning based on land suitability analysis and ecosystem services evaluation: A case study in Liaoning province, China. *Sustainability,* 9, 890.

WANG, Y., MA, J., XIAO, X., WANG, X., DAI, S. & ZHAO, B. 2019. Long-Term Dynamic of Poyang Lake Surface Water: A Mapping Work Based on the Google Earth Engine Cloud Platform. *Remote Sensing,* 11, 313.

WEIH, R. C. & RIGGAN, N. D. 2010. Object-based classification vs. pixel-based classification: Comparative importance of multi-resolution imagery. *The International Archives of the Photogrammetry, Remote Sensing and Spatial Information Sciences,* 38, C7.

WEISS, D. J., NELSON, A., GIBSON, H., TEMPERLEY, W., PEEDELL, S., LIEBER, A., HANCHER, M., POYART, E., BELCHIOR, S. & FULLMAN, N. 2018. A global map of travel time to cities to assess inequalities in accessibility in 2015. *Nature,* 553, 333.

WU, Q., LANE, C. R., LI, X., ZHAO, K., ZHOU, Y., CLINTON, N., DEVRIES, B., GOLDEN, H. E. & LANG, M. W. 2019. Integrating LiDAR data and multi-temporal aerial imagery to map wetland inundation dynamics using Google Earth Engine. *Remote sensing of environment,* 228, 1-13.

XIANZHOU, Z., LING, W., YONGTAO, H., MINGYUAN, D., JING, Z., PEILI, S., CHENGQUN, Y. & YANGJIAN, Z. 2017. Impact of Water Vapor on Elevation-dependent Climate Change. *Journal of resources and ecology,* 8, 5-10.

XIE, S., LIU, L., ZHANG, X., YANG, J., CHEN, X. & GAO, Y. 2019a. Automatic Land-Cover Mapping using Landsat Time-Series Data based on Google Earth Engine. *Remote Sensing,* 11, 3023.

XIE, Z., PHINN, S. R., GAME, E. T., PANNELL, D. J., HOBBS, R. J., BRIGGS, P. R. & MCDONALD-MADDEN, E. 2019b. Using Landsat observations (1988–2017) and Google Earth Engine to detect vegetation cover changes in rangelands-A first step towards identifying degraded lands for conservation. *Remote Sensing of Environment,* 232, 111317.

XIONG, J., THENKABAIL, P., TILTON, J., GUMMA, M., TELUGUNTLA, P., OLIPHANT, A., CONGALTON, R., YADAV, K. & GORELICK, N. 2017a. Nominal 30-m cropland extent map of continental Africa by integrating pixel-based and object-based algorithms using Sentinel-2 and Landsat-8 data on Google Earth Engine. *Remote Sensing,* 9, 1065.

XIONG, J., THENKABAIL, P. S., GUMMA, M. M. K., TELUGUNTLA, P., POEHNELT, J., CONGALTON, R. G., YADAV, K. & THAU, D. 2017b. Automated cropland mapping of continental Africa using Google Earth Engine cloud computing. *ISPRS Journal of Photogrammetry and Remote Sensing,* 126, 225-244.

XIONG, J., THENKABAIL, P. S., TILTON, J. C., GUMMA, M. K., TELUGUNTLA, P., OLIPHANT, A., CONGALTON, R. G., YADAV, K. & GORELICK, N. 2017c. Nominal 30-m cropland extent map of continental Africa by integrating pixel-based and object-based algorithms using Sentinel-2 and Landsat-8 data on Google Earth Engine. *Remote Sensing,* 9, 1065.

XU, E. & ZHANG, H. 2013. Spatially-explicit sensitivity analysis for land suitability evaluation. *Applied Geography,* 45, 1-9.

YADAV, K. & CONGALTON, R. 2018. Accuracy assessment of global food security-support analysis data (GFSAD) cropland extent maps produced at three different spatial resolutions. *Remote Sensing,* 10, 1800.

YALEW, S., VAN GRIENSVEN, A. & VAN DER ZAAG, P. 2016a. AgriSuit: A web-based GIS-MCDA framework for agricultural land suitability assessment. *Computers and Electronics in Agriculture,* 128, 1-8.

YALEW, S. G., VAN GRIENSVEN, A., MUL, M. L. & VAN DER ZAAG, P. 2016b. Land suitability analysis for agriculture in the Abbay basin using remote sensing, GIS and AHP techniques. *Modeling Earth Systems and Environment,* 2, 101.

YU, D., XIE, P., DONG, X., SU, B., HU, X., WANG, K. & XU, S. 2018a. The development of land use planning scenarios based on land suitability and its influences on eco-hydrological responses in the upstream of the Huaihe River basin. *Ecological modelling,* 373, 53-67.

YU, Z., DI, L., TANG, J., ZHANG, C., LIN, L., YU, E. G., RAHMAN, M. S., GAIGALAS, J. & SUN, Z. Land use and land cover classification for Bangladesh 2005 on google earth engine. 2018 7th International Conference on Agro-geoinformatics (Agro-geoinformatics), 2018b. IEEE, 1-5.

YUSRI, S., SIREGAR, V. P. & SUHARSONO, S. GENERATING BIOLOGICALLY RELEVANT ENVIRONMENTAL DATA FROM REMOTE SENSING IMAGERIES AND OCEANOGRAPHIC MODELS TO SUPPORT SPATIAL PRIORITIZATION OF MARINE BIODIVERSITY CONSERVATION AND MANAGEMENT IN INDONESIA. Seminar Nasional Geomatika, 2019. 965-974.

ZABEL, F., PUTZENLECHNER, B. & MAUSER, W. 2014. Global agricultural land resources–a high resolution suitability evaluation and its perspectives until 2100 under climate change conditions. *PloS one,* 9, e107522.

ZAITCHIK, B. F., RODELL, M. & OLIVERA, F. 2010. Evaluation of the Global Land Data Assimilation System using global river discharge data and a source-to-sink routing scheme. *Water Resources Research,* 46.

ZAMAN, N., SELIAMAN, M. E., HASSAN, M. F. & MÁRQUEZ, F. P. G. 2015. *Handbook of Research on Trends and Future Directions in Big Data and Web Intelligence*, Information Science Reference.

ZHANG, J., SU, Y., WU, J. & LIANG, H. 2015. GIS based land suitability assessment for tobacco production using AHP and fuzzy set in Shandong province of China. *Computers and Electronics in Agriculture,* 114, 202-211.

ZHENG, Z., YANG, Z., WU, Z. & MARINELLO, F. 2019. Spatial Variation of NO2 and Its Impact Factors in China: An Application of Sentinel-5P Products. *Remote Sensing,* 11, 1939.

ZIEMKE, J., CHANDRA, S. & BHARTIA, P. 2005. A 25-year data record of atmospheric ozone in the Pacific from Total Ozone Mapping Spectrometer (TOMS) cloud slicing: Implications for ozone trends in the stratosphere and troposphere. *Journal of Geophysical Research: Atmospheres,* 110.

ZOLEKAR, R. B. 2018. Integrative approach of RS and GIS in characterization of land suitability for agriculture: a case study of Darna catchment. *Arabian Journal of Geosciences,* 11, 780.

ZOLEKAR, R. B. & BHAGAT, V. S. 2015. Multi-criteria land suitability analysis for agriculture in hilly zone: Remote sensing and GIS approach. *Computers and Electronics in Agriculture,* 118, 300-321.

ZORAGHEIN, H., LEYK, S., RUTHER, M. & BUTTENFIELD, B. P. 2016. Exploiting temporal information in parcel data to refine small area population estimates. *Computers, Environment and Urban Systems,* 58, 19-28.

ZURQANI, H., POST, C., MIKHAILOVA, E., COPE, M. P., ALLEN, J. & LYTLE, B. Evaluating the integrity of forested riparian buffers over a large area using LiDAR data and Google Earth Engine. Graduate Research and Discovery Symposium (GRADS): Clemson, SC, USA, 2019.

ZURQANI, H. A., POST, C. J., MIKHAILOVA, E. A., SCHLAUTMAN, M. A. & SHARP, J. L. 2018. Geospatial analysis of land use change in the Savannah River Basin using Google Earth Engine. *International journal of applied earth observation and geoinformation,* 69, 175-185.

133

MUHAMMAD UMER received the B.S.C.S. degree from COMSATS University Islamabad Sahiwal, Sahiwal, Pakistan. He is graduated in M.S. degree from COMSATS University Islamabad Sahiwal, Sahiwal, Pakistan. He is currently doing job as a Teacher in Government School of Pakistan. He is also doing a funded project with the government of Pakistan in national research program for universities. His research interests include machine learning, and data sciences.

RANA M. AMIR LATIF received the B.S.C.S. degree from COMSATS University Islamabad Sahiwal, Sahiwal, Pakistan. He is graduated in M.S. degree from COMSATS University Islamabad Sahiwal, Sahiwal, Pakistan. He is currently doing job as a Lecture in Barani Institute of Sciences, Sahiwal. He also had worked as a Lecture of Computer Science at the Quaid-e-Azam College of Engineering and Technology, Sahiwal for about one years. He is also a Research Assistant with the Department of Computer Science, CUI, under the supervision of Dr. M. Farhan. He has many research publications in high impact factor journals also he has many publications in well reputed international conferences. He is also doing a funded project with the government of Pakistan in national research program for universities. His research interests include machine learning, data sciences, and the IoT.

DR. MUHAMMAD FARHAN is working as an Assistant Professor in the Department of Computer Science, COMSATS University Islamabad, Sahiwal Campus, Pakistan. He had worked as a Lecturer in the same department. He completed his Ph.D. in 2017 in the field of Computer Science from the Department of Computer Sciences and Engineering at the University of Engineering and Technology (UET), Pakistan. He obtained MSCS in 2010 from the University of Management and Technology (UMT), Pakistan. He has received BSCS in 2007 from Virtual University of Pakistan (VU). He also had worked as an Instructor of Computer Science at the Virtual University of Pakistan for about 5 years. He started his research career with the publication of a conference paper in San Luis Potosí, Mexico, IEEE CPS. He has honored for winning travel grant provided by ACM and Microsoft for the presentation of a student paper in the ACM/SIGAPP Symposium (Human-Computer Interaction track) held by the University of Salamanca, Spain. He has published a good number of SCI-indexed impact factor journal papers, which are published by Journal of Real-Time Image Processing by Springer, Multimedia Tools and Applications by Springer, International Journal of Distributed Sensor Networks by SAGE Journals, EURASIA Journal of Mathematics, Science and Technology Education by MODESTUM, Life Science Journal by Marshland Press and in various renowned journals of IEEE, Springer, Elsevier and Hindawi. His interests include Data Science, machine & deep learning, and Internet of Things.

Dr Noor Zaman Jhanjhi is currently working as Associate Professor with Taylor's University Malaysia. He has great international exposure in academia, research, administration, and academic quality accreditation. He worked with ILMA University, and King Faisal University (KFU) for a decade. He has 20 years of teaching & administrative experience. He has an intensive background of academic quality accreditation in higher education besides scientific research activities, he had worked a decade for academic accreditation and earned ABET accreditation twice for three programs at CCSIT, King Faisal University, Saudi Arabia. He also worked for National Commission for Academic Accreditation and Assessment (NCAAA), Education Evaluation Commission Higher Education Sector (EECHES) formerly NCAAA Saudi Arabia, for institutional level accreditation. He also worked for the National Computing Education Accreditation Council (NCEAC).

Dr Noor Zaman has awarded as top reviewer 1% globally by WoS/ISI (Publons) recently for the year 2019. He has edited/authored more than 13 research books with international reputed publishers, earned several research grants, and a great number of indexed research articles on his credit. He has supervised several postgraduate students, including master's and PhD. Dr Noor Zaman Jhanjhi is an Associate Editor of IEEE ACCESS, moderator of IEEE TechRxiv, Keynote speaker for several IEEE international conferences globally, External examiner/evaluator for PhD and masters for several universities, Guest editor of several reputed journals, member of the editorial board of several research journals, and active TPC member of reputed conferences around the globe.

Dr Mamoona Humayun has completed her PhD. in Computer Architecture from  Harbin Institute of Technology, China. She has 12 years of teaching and administrative experience internationally. She is an active reviewer for a series of journals. She has supervised various master's and Ph.D. thesis. Her research interests include Global software development, requirement engineering, knowledge management, Cyber Security, and wireless sensor networks.

Dr Syed Jawad Hussain completed his B.S. with major in Mathematics in 1999. He  received the master's in computer science degree from International Islamic University, Islamabad, Pakistan in 2002. He worked in the industry for five years as embedded system developer. He did Postgraduate diploma from Massey University in 2009 and PhD in 2015 in computer networks. Currently working as Associate Professor in barani institute of information technology, BIIT, PMAS, Arid Agriculture University Rawalpindi. His Current research interest includes machine learning, e-Learning and cyber security.

Publisher: Eliva Press SRL

Email: info@elivapress.com